Blue Ball Syndrome:

Why Ordinary People Become Sexual Players

Dr. John E. Bell

RIVERHOUSE PUBLISHING

Blue Ball Syndrome:
Why Ordinary People Become Sexual Players

RiverHouse Publishing, LLC
5100 Poplar Avenue
Suite 2700
Memphis, TN 38117

Copyright © 2011 by Dr. John E. Bell

All rights reserved. No part of this book may be reproduced, stored in a retrieval system or transmitted in any form or by any means without written permission of the Publisher, excepting brief quotes used in reviews.

All **RiverHouse, LLC** Titles, Imprints and Distributed Lines are available at special quantity discounts for bulk purchases for sales promotions, premiums, fund-raising and educational or institutional use.

First RiverHouse, LLC Trade Paperback Printing: 10/24/2011

1 2

ISBN 978-0-9839819-2-3

Printed in the United States of America

This book is printed on acid-free paper.

www.riverhousepublishingllc.com

This book is dedicated to all people that want to find someone special in their lives but have endured countless rejection and humiliation from nonproductive relationships. This book is also dedicated to women who feel all men are dogs and that all the good men are either married or gay or may be even on the down low. This book is to demonstrate that many good women and good men consistently miss each other as their lives always seem to cross with passion and the occasional arousal that would indicate good consensual sexual enjoyment.

However, this book highlights the experiences of sexual arousal and preparation for moment of sexual pleasure all to be dismissed by a man or woman that limits the moment or does not allow the moment to happen at all. This type of crisis that interrupts the moment of sexual stimulation that keeps men and women from reaching the moment of orgasm and release of the bodily fluid that this scenario produces are detrimental to the sexes physical and psychological state of health.

This phenomenon is called Blue Ball Syndrome and no man or woman enjoys this arousal without completion of sexual enjoyment. Ironically, women are susceptible to this syndrome as well but it is usually called something different such as "hot and bothered with no relief of orgasm." There are so many names for these unfortunate events in life, however one must know what is happening in order to fix a problem that is occurring in a relationship. It is my personal hope that this book will help many people realize how to relax and enjoy life's little moments of pleasure be it sexually, mentally or in an act of kindness.

Furthermore, we will discover that we do not have time to be petty when it comes to life's opportunity for pleasure and gratification of the beautiful moments we cherish. Moreover, we will see that these special times are opportunities for moving mankind forward and without the pleasures of orgasm and quality of time being spent relationships die and become lifeless or boring. It is in this effort that I hope all who read this can find comfort in the fact that life itself can be pleasurable and often a painful experience as well.

However, it is nothing without someone to share both of those times with especially when one can help provide pleasure and smooth issues out until challenging times improve. Sexual pleasure is humanity's release valve from life's daily pressures that we all have. If an orgasm is denied, life becomes miniscule and meaningless and Blue Ball Syndrome replaces living.

Acknowledgments

I want to thank my friends and family for all of their love and support on this project, without them I could not do what I love to do in my life. I dedicate this project to my daughter, family, friends and colleagues who find life often cruel or misunderstood from a human's perspective of life's challenges from my view point. I will add that I also dedicate this project to men and women in their own life that will ask how life can be so challenging without many opportunities to share some pleasure from life's daily trials. It is my personal hope that this project of love from my heart soothes the burden of the grind of life's challenges in finding a good relationship and one day even a good marriage for your life.

To my daughter Amber that will be too young to read this for many years, I say that life is short but sweet and good to those who learn the secret of God's plan early and rely on true love and wisdom to lead them throughout their lives. It is a blessing to have a guide from love and life's experiences, use it and meditate on it so your path will be bright and your life less confusing as your journey begins in your own search for love, life and happiness. Finally, I want to gratefully thank Dr. Sigmund McIntyre for reediting this literary published work. I wish all who read this book to aspire for life's wonderful joys and cherish loved ones who exist in our lives daily. It is only then that relationships make sense in the ever evolving pace of life which is sustainable by having good love and memorable moments with each other.

Blue Ball Syndrome:

Why Ordinary People Become Sexual Players

Table of Contents

Chapter 1 1
Chapter 2 7
Chapter 3 18
Chapter 4 36
Chapter 5 47
Chapter 6 81
Chapter 7 86
Chapter 8 92
Chapter 9 97
Chapter 10 105
Chapter 11 118
Chapter 12 126
Chapter 13 142
Chapter 14 152
Chapter 15 164
Chapter 16 187

Chapter 1

WHAT IS BLUE BALL SYNDROME?

Blue Balls is a medical term that has been coined for a man that has vascular congestion of the testes due to heightened excitement but no release of the sperm from the vesicles in the testes, also known as an ejaculation. This can be quite complicated in a man's psychological state since most men are physical and visual and the emotional status of a man follows his satisfaction of how he can interact with a woman.

Ironically, guys will always have a deceptive mechanism not to tell a woman that they are having blue balls when they cannot have sex with a female. Most men do not want to disappoint a woman or turn her off from being too aggressive in their search for sex.

Women can have Blue Ball Syndrome as well when not routinely sexually active with a man; this builds stress in women psychologically and escalates anxiety as well. I must point out for clarity sake that women do not have testicles as men do but can experience Blue Ball Syndrome psychologically just as men do.

Most women may not see this phenomenon the same as a man and that's due to the fact that most females are emotional and bond with time with the course of how a man approaches her to persuade the female of his sincerity and depth of feelings.

Women are open to great conversation and honesty in the pursuer in his efforts to be a short time lover, a one night stand or possibly the real deal that could lead to marriage.

However, in men this is the contrast that makes men different from women. Men, in general are more physical and appearance driven creatures of what we can feel and touch and for the most part interact with like a toy.

Men love affection and have an affinity for a female that can please her man with her charm and her creation of his personality that attracts all men to women. Most men love comments, even if they play it off, they love it. It makes them feel more prone to be attracted to a female that other men would like to pursue.

It has been said by many experts that if a woman knew her power over her man by appealing to his manhood then that woman would rule that mans world. When a man has planned to pursue a female and has put that female in his target of pleasure, the male pursuer becomes a lion after a prey and his imagination and efforts are to experience this woman and express himself with all of his heart. Honestly, this can be a vulnerable place for a man.

If you are pursuing a person and that person declines an appropriate conversation, it is a disappointment to anyone.

Blue Ball Syndrome

This is not a good experience for either men or women and will often make a person feel awkward or even end a relationship before one can even begin.

In my friend Torrey's case, he planned to be with a beautiful young lady one evening that he met about two weeks ago at a local business party. The lady was beautiful in his eyes and could do no wrong to Torrey; she was dating material and possibly what he has been looking for all his life.

I felt good for him and it had been awhile since he had pursued a young lady to this extent. I could certainly tell that he was totally feeling this young lady as he told me about their phone conversations. I remember how they were planning on having a wonderful evening together with a great dinner and dancing to top it off. It all sounded great and I could not be happier for the guy. I knew Torrey was looking for something stable in his life and a year before meeting this young lady he had a bad break up from a previous girlfriend.

Therefore, to see him happy again was a great thing indeed. Torrey came to my house illuminating as if a bright light was beaming off of him and I wished him the best on his date with this new young lady. Torrey left and began his date with his young lady and all went well.

However, Torrey told me that when he arrived at the meeting place to meet this young lady she was late and dinner at the restaurant that he picked out that night was not the best of service.

It appeared that all was not going well, until finally his girlfriend arrived and looked stunning. She was tuned into Torrey and assured him that she was sorry that the subway made her arrive a little later than she expected.

The young lady assured Torrey that the restaurant was great even though the service was a little slow that night. The young lady grabbed Torrey's hand as the night music played and asked him to dance and Torrey was just overjoyed to be in his date's presence. Torrey actually had a great time with her and felt so blessed to be right there at that moment, he wanted to be no other place.

As the music played and the couple held each other close Torrey felt his manhood rise and his date felt it as well. But she did not back away from his erect penis and he felt even closer to her for that. In his mind, he felt that he found the greatest thing ever and only wished that it would last forever.

Torrey admitted his date smelled great and her hair was thick and long and hanging down her back. Torrey's date had on a one-piece dress that fitted great, not too tight or too revealing. She was totally Torrey's type of woman and for once I was happy for him.   The couple enjoyed dinner and had a wonderful evening. All was well.

The evening was growing to a close and the happy couple began to head for home and Torrey drove his date home to her apartment. He walked her to the doorstep and he told her that he had a great time, she agreed that it was a great evening as well.

Torrey was very sexually stimulated and his penis was hard at this time and he knew that he wanted to make love to this woman but he did not want to be aggressive about how he felt. He did not want to spoil such a wonderful evening that he had experienced.

His date was sensing his attraction for her and the moment was hot and heavy on her as well. However, neither one of the two wanted to say anything or seem like either one was being too easy to get or acting like sex was the only thing that they wanted from each other. Finally, after kissing passionately and feeling the warmth of the woman on his body, passions escalated like a burning fire that lights up the soul.

As a gesture of breaking the moment, Torrey's date gently told Torrey passionately, "Torrey, I had a great time and I am so happy that we went out tonight and I would love to go out with you again sometime soon. I want you to know that I am so attracted to you so I am hoping if we do not have sex tonight that it will not ruin this moment right now."

Torrey replied, "not at all, I am just glad that you enjoyed me as much as I enjoyed you and I would love to see you again as well. I will not lie, I want you sexually but I want you more just knowing that we will have something wonderful for the next time we see each other."

The couple kissed passionately and then the beautiful young lady hugged and kissed Torrey one last time and then went inside her apartment.

Torrey could feel his penis sticking out through his boxers and knew he would develop the Blue Ball Syndrome since he was so excited over his dating experience because of having no sexual stimulation to release an orgasm. But who cares about the blue balls when the heart is happy, you have done the right thing and have not spoiled a potentially great relationship.

Torrey knows now that he wants that girl ten times greater than before his date tonight even with a mild case of Blue Ball Syndrome that ironically made this night turn out just fine.

Chapter 2

WHY DO GOOD PEOPLE BECOME SEXUAL PLAYERS?

First, to answer this question thoroughly we must analyze what a good person is in our discussion of what may lead such a person to become a sexual player.

Although it is always assumed that all men are dogs or they are not heartfelt beings that can treat women well, I have lived to disagree with this statement and many of the statements that would usually accompany this one. I know firsthand that all men are not dogs and most men do not start their lives out with thuggish natures and cold hearts toward women.

Quite the contrary to popular belief, most men are very eager to please women and honestly want to find the right woman to fit into the man's world; ironically, this will complete his journey toward being the man that he truly desires to be.

When men first begin to seek women to date, they seek a worthy, real, lasting relationship that can truly open them up from the inside and allow them to feel the woman and the essence of who she is. Men are touch and feel creatures and bond to woman by smell, touch, sight and often taste.

The reality of how a man visualizes women is deeply comparable to how male ancestors must have been attracted to females.

This is usually by the fragrance of a female's natural smell and the feel of her skin. The sight of a fine female with the contour of her breast, shape of her thighs, fullness of her hips and lips, and also her eyes would stimulate a special hormonal reaction of sexual arousal in men.

In the evolution of man that has occurred over thousands of years however, one characteristic in humanity has remained, to be physically satisfied by the opposite sex. This internal craving of sexuality predicts how men judge levels of relationships with their female companions.

Occasionally, men are aroused for sex even if not touching a female in a relationship. This causes a physical testosterone stimulation that indicates a female is of high importance.

Uniquely, for men, as their arousal reaches the ecstasy level, this relates to the physical sensation of an orgasm with ejaculation. The man establishes his feelings and his heart is suddenly captured and we all know of our human story evolving around such an event.

Objectively, when a man has reached this place of reception for a particular female and that female does not respond to the man with the same zeal or intimate affection as this very malleable individual male, unfortunately, the heart of the man is ill served and his open heart begins to close slowly in areas of vulnerability. This leads to division and separatism between the couples and the thrill and elation of such a wonderful intimate event now becomes an embarrassment. This spiral eventful downfall becomes the bitterness of the heart of a man and the dying innocence of romance and intimacy with their female counterpart. This is the same with women as well. In most people, the wonder of love and true passion does exist, however this special place can be polluted by negative emotional experiences that alters the heart of a person and yields a vulnerable, empty soul.

This formerly good person in heart yet has good in them but life's disappointments and self inflicted failures of self expectation take a toll on anyone especially when that nice person was all about finding a stable and optimistic individual to share their world with. This is the evolution of how a good man can become self absorbed and distant in heart toward women that they will encounter in their future.

In comparison, women also go through this open heart phase in their lives as well and eventually develop similar characteristics of emotional detachment and deceptive tactics, these keep the women from truly being a target for men who prey on young, tender and vulnerable hearted women that are open targets for the former good men of society.

Our next case scenario begins as we evaluate the life of Brad who used to be a great guy and optimistic about love and great relationships. Brad is a good friend who is dating a young lady that he met at college. Brad is college educated, he has an undergraduate BS degree in Biology from Tuskegee University and a Masters degree from Ohio State University in Bioengineering, he has a great job in Atlanta as a Bioengineer with the DuPont Corporation. Brad earns around $85,000 a year with outstanding benefits and has no children, he is well built and has a great church background. Brad also has a great talent for dressing casual and living life. He has his own apartment and he is heterosexual.

Brad has it going on and he would be labeled as a good guy by many female standards indeed. Brad is currently dating Cheyenne who is a smooth, brown-skinned lovely African-American female that has her BS degree in Criminal Justice from Ohio State University and is from Birmingham, Alabama.

Cheyenne is an adventurous, well built woman with beautiful eyes. She is a tall, slender type woman with a great smile and lovely natural shoulder length hair. She is currently finishing up her Masters degree in Criminal Law and hopes to join the FBI or CIA when she has completed her education. So she is also very driven and capable of obviously being a great woman of stature and would be seen as good in many men's eyes.

The question would be how could these two well educated and seemingly well rounded individuals miss each other or the opportunity to make life a good reality for each other? As we look further, the answer of how a good man becomes a sexual player will become apparent as we journey further into the lives of these two seemingly perfect people. It is often said, "That if you feel that you have found perfection in a person then give that person a heavenly crown because they must not be a person from earth they have to be from heaven."

Brad is crazy about Cheyenne and why shouldn't he be. Cheyenne is beautiful, intelligent and fun to be with, she also comes from a similar Christian background as Brad and she also goes to the same graduate school as Brad so, what is the problem with them becoming a great couple? Brad is looking for a great woman to settle down with and have a great life to enjoy.

Cheyenne, is yet adventurous and she is yet experiencing the out of Alabama phenomenon that many people experience when they leave small rural communities in the south and experience big city college campus life with a large diversity of people and not just Black and White cultural dominance.

Brad enjoys being out with Cheyenne and kissing her is a real treat but one thing is always noticed by Brad when he tries to kiss Cheyenne, she does not like to kiss him in public. It makes Brad feel a sense of division between them and it also makes him feel that Cheyenne is not totally feeling him as passionately as he is into her.

He tries not to make a big deal about it but it always happens when they are in public and when he feels like it would be appropriate to show affection to Cheyenne.

Cheyenne often says, "Brad I like kissing you too but, I don't want to make a scene in the street with you." Brad often does not know how to take what Cheyenne says about kissing the man that she supposed to love and he develops mixed emotions about this.

Cheyenne also gets many phone calls throughout the evening that Brad spends with her. It is often annoying to Brad and he asked her about it. Brad asked, "Cheyenne why do you have guys calling you so late when we are together and are establishing our relationship?"

Cheyenne responds by saying, "Brad I can get phone calls anytime, I pay the bill and my guy friends get off work late sometimes about 10:30pm or 11:45pm at night so it is the only time that they can call me." Brad often feels mad at that response and finds himself with very little to say because Cheyenne does pay for her own phone bills.

Cheyenne also is the person that is very outgoing and has sort of an open door policy with her friends. Brad is not Mr. Perfect of this scenario; Cheyenne often accuses him of not listening to her when she talks about her day and what is going on with her life.

Brad tries to follow her conversation about what makes Cheyenne tick but it is a bit distant from

Blue Ball Syndrome

what he does in engineering and he finds it often boring. Brad is not into Cheyenne's criminal studies as she is and unfortunately, Cheyenne picks up on that boredom and she does not like the cold shoulder from Brad on what she likes.

As we can clearly see, Brad and Cheyenne are great on paper but in reality they are friction and divisive to each other. However, this is not in harmful major ways but definitely in a small annoying way that actually leads to doubt and loss of interest in any relationship.

Cheyenne cares for Brad and tries to share some great intimate time with Brad. Brad loves the behind closed door effect of Cheyenne she can really turn on the sexy and erotic allure that really turns Brad on. Cheyenne knows how to please Brad by her touch and her kiss that is not equaled at all by any woman that Brad has ever known. Cheyenne enjoys Brad's energy and his masculine physique and his ability to go out of his way to please her sexually and Brad is eager to please her at all times.

The sex is incredible between Brad and Cheyenne and he is never unsatisfied. Cheyenne is a person that likes to cuddle and be held and talk after sex and she is totally opposite from the outside world under the covers and behind closed doors.

Brad is always satisfied by Cheyenne but he gets off work after a 9 hour day and he is tired often during the week so the cuddling and the talking after sex the way Cheyenne likes it is often no first on his priority list of things to accompany Cheyenne with. Cheyenne deals with this but Brad is not into her as she is into him sexually and begins to withdraw her affection slowly from Brad. Moreover, Brad is noticing that his sessions of sexual bliss are beginning to diminish and become ever infrequent between the two of them.

One day, Brad is on his way to the office and notices a good lady friend from back in the day. Her name is Lisa and she is in town for a conference that will last a few days.   Brad knows Lisa very well because they used to be sexual buddies back in the day in his early years of college and Lisa was also a great sexual experience to Brad.

Lisa was available and the attraction that Lisa and Brad once had suddenly gave way to the opportunity of sexual gratification to be had between the two of them. Besides, Lisa already knew that Brad was not married but she knew he was simply out for some ass and Lisa was out for some dick so they already understood what an evening meant for the two of them so getting it on sexually was easy.

Brad begins to think about Cheyenne as he prepared in his mind to have some good ole no strings attached sex with Lisa.

Brad began to think of all the negative times that she made him feel distant from her like her late night phone calls from men and her not wanting to kiss him in public. Brad began to think of how Cheyenne would be on the dance floor with him and he would catch her looking at other men.

Blue Ball Syndrome

Cheyenne would often not want Brad to hold her on the dance floor, as if she did not know him. Brad would get so pissed off at this that he really became quite in different with going out with her. Consequently, Brad knew that Cheyenne most likely had someone else other than him but he could not prove that with evidence, but a man usually knows this by how he is being treated.

With all this emotional distancing going on in Brad's mind he decides that being with Lisa is a revenge fuck and Lisa loved to go down and give great head to Brad back in the days. Hell, Lisa would swallow his cum and massage his dick and relax his back muscles with a passionate massage. Brad only hoped that she still had that skill that he could totally use from his mental abuse that he had suffered in his mind from Cheyenne. Men love revenge fucks especially when they are from someone else and not the person that they are with.

It is the door that opens in a man's mind when a woman is not treating him right especially when the man's sex is withheld or the excitement of the sexual relationship is gone.

In contrast, Cheyenne did have a player moment as well and she had a side man that was one of her men friends who called her at night and she liked him because he was not a pretty boy like Brad, he was a wanna be gangsta type that did not have the emotional attachment like Brad.

Cheyenne's mystery guy merely wanted to stick the dick as far as it could go in the vaginal canal and fuck the shit out of Cheyenne for about 20 minutes.

Cheyenne would wrap her lovely shapely thighs and legs around her lover and squeeze him deeper in the warm juices of her abyss that craved this man. At the climax of her orgasm and his maximizing thrust of passion in her sexual missionary position, the mystery man would lay on top of her not to put his weight on her but merely lying in her wet vaginal juices and telling her how beautiful she was as he stroked her natural shoulder length hair.

This would make her have an orgasm even when her mystery man was already relaxed and had cum into the condom that was usually stretched to the max deep inside Cheyenne. This shows us that Blue Ball Syndrome does not always have to be physical, it can also be mental and this is usually when both people are involved in a relationship outside of their own. This revelation can be disastrous if anyone gets hurt and the truth of loneliness and disgust of the other partner is revealed.

Brad and Cheyenne are experiencing the end of their relationship with Blue Ball Syndrome that has driven each of them apart and into the inherent search of sexual satisfaction. This scenario does not have a race on it or a gender that is exclusive to it. All nationalities of humanity and sexual orientations are open to the opportunity of sexual frustration when one or both parties in a relationship divide the core of the mental and physical need of intimacy of the other partner.

Blue Ball Syndrome

It is often a gradual process that eventually in its fruition devours most relationships that are not capable of remaining intact with communication and basic understanding of the relationship.

Blue Ball Syndrome is clearly the psychological diagnosis of a process that drives the emotions and actions of a frustrated individual that is wounded usually for lack of sexual satisfaction and intimacy both physically and mentally in a relationship as we have witnessed with Brad and Cheyenne. Unfortunately, this is how good well educated and even the religious church going men and women can become sexual players.

Chapter 3

WHY MEN HATE SEXUAL TEASERS

This chapter hopes to define the rationale of why certain people have an issue with persons who play games and actually frustrate good people with sexual interludes that never manifest into the satisfaction of sexual gratification for a man to enjoy the woman and vice-versa. First, men are creatures of what they can touch, feel, taste and hold. Usually, in the mating game, the hormonal testosterone level in a man guides his motives for satisfaction and sexual gratification. It is the physical build and pheromones of the female that are the attractant formula for the males to females and it is also the driving force of why men like to be promiscuous and even flirtatious with women in order to fill the male testosterone behavior of seeking the female phenomenon.

This has dictated why many males seek a sexual partner with heighten arousal that becomes that special one the man endlessly pursues. Men build up a high amount of energy and excitement when preparing to engage women into a sexual encounter or interlude of a sexual relationship. Many men are very visual and actually see the female imagery in their minds as they contemplate the actual setting

Blue Ball Syndrome

of how the sexual encounter will play out. It is commonly known that men are usually very aroused even erected at those mental images of the female and this excites not only the male physically but actually stimulates the anticipation of orgasm in his mind, this can often make a man ejaculate, often prematurely before the female touches the male or first embraces or even kisses the man. Furthermore, this arousal is an opportunity that allows men to spread his genes or even enjoy the satisfaction of sexual intimacy.

In many instances, men are the most pursuant of the opportunity to seek the female for sexual activity and it seems that in many cases this has been the case for thousands of years. It has been highly studied about the behavior of what attracts a man to a woman and the cultural attributes of the search for the right female is the plight that most young males from age 16 to 75 have to conquer in their lifetimes. This is known as the need to procreate and have babies and multiply.

According to human behavior, over the evolvement of mankind, one would think that mankind in our way of life has changed from this mission but that is simply not the case. The laws have changed and the consequences of how men are expected to provide care of their offspring has changed for the better. However, the primitive pursuit of the satisfaction of the opposite sex has remained abundant and active in the male because of the hormone testosterone.

Now we have discovered what drives a man to seek a female and what all goes into the cultural ceremony of sexual promiscuity among the sexes.

It can be clear now why people hate sexual interludes that do not manifest into sexual satisfaction of an orgasm from a neutral perspective. I must clarify for the sake of the reader that by no means do I suggest the support of indecent proposals that should be entertained by a female from a male.

Quite naturally, if any woman declines sexual activity with a man, then the man should respect that females right to not engage in that activity with her and simply move on about his business. I do not support rape or forced coercion of any kind from male to female or for that matter of any minors with adults as well.

I am simply stating what many men feel when they are good guys who are teased with sex by a female that they are interested in or have established a relationship which makes many men mad as hell at the woman for being a sexual tease with no action or sexual satisfaction.

Both sexes hate being teased with the activity of sexual gratification when the actual moment is withheld and this non-response brings on frustration and Blue Ball Syndrome. Men are often angry when they have planned and actually have placed great emphasis on this level of a relationship with a woman and the woman turns out to be a person that simply talks up a moment of sexual activity to only leave the man with his arousal but no completion of sexual satisfaction. As you can see, the hormonal level in males creates the moment of stimulation even with the thought pattern of men as they entertain the female about this aspect of a relationship.

I have found after talking to many of my good friends that are heterosexual and single that they handle the female teaser in a different way than even a female who is more open and sexually responsible to experience this sexual interlude with. It is unrealistic for people to expect a great sexual, mature experience from a person that is not at their level of anticipation of the moment.

This unfortunately leads to immaturity with sexual games by someone that an open-minded mature person is not seeking to entertain. This none congenial moment would ultimately present frustration to any man or woman because of their mental preparedness and expectation of a moment they are prepared for.

However, the immature individual is not properly matched with the same level of acceptance from this person the pursuer is entertaining. This divides the best of relationships and in ones own mind they feel differently about each other, occasionally, for the worst and not the better of the relationship. Men and women both hate to be teased sexually in their minds when the body and the mind are aroused and ready for the moment.

For example, if you ever had a moment that you were anticipating someone to experience a sexual encounter with and you were really into entertaining this special person, you would actually get your body prepared with a warm shower with your favorite scented soap. If you are doing this at your own home then you would usually get the food prepared or order some food in.

You know you cannot have incredible sex on an empty stomach, that is no fun, trust me. You would clean the house and make the setting for the experience immaculate, there would be no children around because you would take them over to your relative's home or get a babysitter for a few hours. Women would also sometimes get their hair done and for men we would cut our hair to look good with a line and all.

For some men they would get a nice hotel where everything was already laid out. Men who are responsible will also purchase some KY gel and latex condoms and have it either in the drawer next to the bed or under the pillow and prepare for the mature sexual experience.

I am finding that some females like to go the hotel route as well not only to have a great sexual experience but also to keep the person from knowing where they live. This cuts out creeping to their door step unannounced. You always know if it is good to your special lover, they could get hooked on your good stuff if you know how to lay it down right.

Blue Ball Syndrome

Well, let me stop digressing and get to my point. In all of this preparedness for a mature sexual encounter with a person that you are feeling for at this level, the maturity factor shows who can handle this type of activity.

As one can relate to the anticipation of the person that was mature about this preparation for such a sexual encounter, then one would have to feel the frustration when the individual finally shows up after this preparation and they are not readily mature as the moment calls for them to be. Consequently, this person only presents with games and immaturity and simply spoils the whole damn moment with their lack of sexual maturity for the experience.

Honestly, I have not talked to one individual yet that has not experienced an immature person that naturally and simply was a tease or immature to the moment sexual satisfaction. You feel like throwing them out like trash on the street for wasting your time and not being considerate of the moment in such a way after you made all the preparations.

I think everyone can feel this level of frustration that one feels from such an experience. It adds credibility to why people hate sexual teasers who talk a good game but cannot back it up. This is immature and leaves the pursuer frustrated, ready to move on.

Now, do not get teased mixed up with a person that is withholding a sexual encounter from the right person to not cause frustration to the ordinary people amongst us.

There is a difference and we will look at that difference and examine it closely as well. One important difference is that men or women who are mature about themselves first of all will not tease you at all. They will be honest and up front about where they stand on many topics as it relates to sexuality and usually will let you know where they stand. Most men and women will also let you know how they want that experience to occur.

Ironically, the person that is more upfront and can converse maturely about the subject of sexual pleasure is usually the most prepared for such an experience to occur.

Mature people are usually waiting on the right person to entertain there way of sex where discretion and confidence can be maintained. In contrast, I have found that it is the person who talks up a good game about what they can do to you and how good their sex is typically that has the most unrealistic chance of being mature sexually about such a grown up situation.

It sounds like they want to put your mind on a teasing point with no substance to enjoy such a moment and this begins the whole frustration that divides good people who know how to be mature and prepare for what they want.

Moreover, this type of person who does talk a good game and yet can not back his or her mouth up is the same individual that tries to know it all about what others should do in their relationships. Consequently, this type of person usually gossips and is never in a lengthy relationship themselves. This very shallow immature individual can never totally give their heart to anyone for love due to innate selfishness and the inability to respect another person, it is against the very nature of these immature souls.

If one is ever involved in a relationship with an immature person of this magnitude be prepared to be in a short relationship. You will rarely get any mental or physical satisfaction from this person. Ironically, as for sexual satisfaction, masturbation is usually more satisfying than an evening filled with games and immaturity from a person that looks like an adult but is yet held back in the school of youth in their mind and unfortunately causes Blue Ball Syndrome naturally to occur.

This brings us to my good friend Cynthia and her immature man, Phillip. Cynthia is a great friend of mine, we go back about two years when I met her at a conference in Washington, D.C. Cynthia is a graduate of Grambling State University with a Master's degree in Public Health and Business. She is an administrator with the US Department of Agriculture out of D.C. and has a great career.

When I met Cynthia she was with her man Phillip who is also an administrator with the Agricultural Department in Human Resources in D.C. as well. I thought that they were the perfect couple, just to look at them you would never think that

Cynthia who is age 31 with no children would have man problems in her life. Cynthia is very attractive with long natural hair past her shoulders and a very pretty golden brown skin tone, beautiful brown eyes and a great smile. She weighs about 130 pounds and is 5'7" tall. Many guys would call her a model easily and most do out of her presence. It is very sad that a woman so lovely not only in beauty but in spirit would smile in public with her man but inside would be experiencing the Blue Ball Syndrome from her man, Phillip.

Conversely, Phillip is not very mature in his relationship with Cynthia, he is often reluctant to take her out and share his emotion in public with Cynthia. Cynthia is usually the one making all of their outgoing plans. Cynthia is a very social butterfly that likes to dance and she loves the arts like stage production with Tyler Perry production style plays, great movies and book readings, she is also a great community person and she volunteers with Big Sisters of D.C.

Cynthia is a member of Delta Sigma Theta Sorority Inc. and she is also very active in her local graduate chapter. Phillip is the complete opposite, he rarely goes out and is a more conservative person that likes to attend all the free activities, he does not like to spend any money when he goes out. It is a clash of the titans when Cynthia goes out with him, she likes to attend some fund raising activities for worthy causes such as March of Dimes and Phillip could care less. He is always finding

Blue Ball Syndrome

some complaint about giving his money for some cause as if someone is always out for his money. Phillip is an attractive guy, brown skin, tall about 5'11" and he weighs about 190 pounds, he is built very well and works out about 3 times a week. Phillip, to be as selfish as he is, has no problems attracting women. It is keeping women in a relationship with him that is his problem.

Clearly, we can see Phillip's type of personality is a divisive wedge already between himself and Cynthia. Ironically, when I met Cynthia and Phillip, I happened to hear about their frustration at my table as they were seated right behind me and I know others heard them but did not bother the disagreeing couple. I was a speaker that day and after I spoke to the audience Cynthia and Phillip approached me about some meeting potentials for their organizations.

I agreed to meet with their departments and in the meantime I invited them to join me for lunch at my table. As usual, I was trying to depressurize their confrontation and it worked, they got back into their professional roles with me at the table and all was relaxed again.

Consequently, Phillip and Cynthia were curious about me and asked if I was married and I told them that I was and had a family. In exchange, I asked about them and their relationship. I could see that Phillip was uncomfortable about talking to me about their relationship but Cynthia was ready and seemed to be looking for someone to talk with.

Furthermore, I could see how unhappy she was and she was definitely experiencing Blue Ball Syndrome. Phillip could naturally see her frustration with him and it was apparent that they were good ordinary people, both professionals and both of them looked like the perfect couple together. However, a critical element was missing between them and it came down to Phillip being selfish and his lack of maturity to correct his boyhood mannerism for his relationship with Cynthia.

Unfortunately, Cynthia was dying inside because she really cared for Phillip but he was not responding to the woman that Cynthia was or more importantly to the woman that needed nourishing. Cynthia began to tell me that Phillip did not like to be out in public with her to show affection and he would always walk in front of her and not hold her hand in public as if he had a side affair that he did not want someone to know about. Of course, Phillip denied all these allegations but Cynthia hit his nerve when she confessed to me that Phillip held back sexually as if he did not like her bedroom fantasies.

Phillip, said, "Why are you putting that out there Cynthia, you do not even know this dude that is between us, what is up with that girl?"

I replied, "Phillip, you are making a scene now and you are at my table as my guest. What you do at your table is your business but brother, you are at my table now and if you cannot control yourself

Blue Ball Syndrome

out of respect for me then you need to excuse yourself!"

Phillip then got up and left from the table, I could see that Cynthia had tears in her eyes and felt relieved that Phillip left the table. Cynthia and I sat at my table and had a great conversation, I could tell that she had been waiting for this moment to express herself and I listened to her as she told me about what her life was like. Cynthia allowed me to enter her world. It seemed, according to her, that Phillip was mentally abusive towards her by not allowing Cynthia to express herself or not compromising his desires for what Cynthia wanted.

For example, Cynthia enjoyed taking a warm shower or a warm bath in the evening and just having Phillip there to provide a massage and some gentle quiet time after a hard day. According to Cynthia, this is great to her but Phillip only wants to shower, very rarely does he even listen to her when they are in her apartment, it seems Phillip only wants her to do his sexual business simply missionary, leading to no foreplay or satisfaction for her at all.

As I listened to Cynthia, I could see that she was really as lonely as I had been at one time in my own life. It also allowed me to relate to her about who Phillip really was. Cynthia already knew the answer of how insecure and immature Phillip was. Cynthia never really thought about doing anything about it because Cynthia was afraid to be alone. She had felt the sting of loneliness that many women and men have felt in her situation as well. It feels almost like an invisible prison where you want to have sexual pleasure and enjoy a mature person that you really like. But that person is not attentive or does not know how to unlock the door to where your special place is in your prison of loneliness. This situation can sometimes be a real shame in relationships.

Consequently, this situation had closed in on Cynthia and her sex life and fantasies of a good man to love and rapture her were fading fast. It was as if she loved a man but the man did not love her enough to want her satisfied above himself and that was a problem. Phillip was this man in her life and it was him for now or deal with being alone and at home with no one to call or no one to take you out. Cynthia dreaded that no one would at least hold her sometimes even if it is a brief moment, you know at least you would have someone.

These were the words from Cynthia and it reminded me of many of my words that I have said in my own life as I looked in life's mirror as all people do and see themselves getting older and chubbier through the years.

It seems that loneliness is a real fear that actually makes many men and women take a somebody in their life even if that somebody is not the ultimate person to makes them happy and that is where Cynthia was in her life.

She was 31, almost 32 and to her that was getting old because she had no children, was never married or shared any real bond with any man. Phillip was her first real steady relationship, this she realized now after dating in the past and having her heart broken.

Cynthia now is getting older in her mind and desperate, she wants to commit to someone special in life. Naturally, to Cynthia it seems that Phillip is the closest thing that she has come to a man that is not bi-sexual or homosexual.

Ironically, in D.C., the HIV rate is estimated to be one out of every seven African-American men and Cynthia does not want that man to enter her life. Therefore, as an African-American woman in D.C. and getting older and facing all these statistics, Phillip may not seem like a bad match. He is heterosexual and HIV negative, he has his education and a great career with the Agricultural department. He is also a great dresser and very articulate.

However, he is a cancer to the spirit of Cynthia. Until she realizes that she is worth more than someone of his selfish controlling ways she will never be happy and unfortunately will never know what real relationship happiness is all about at that level of intimacy with someone special.

This is a real life crisis not only for women but also for men as well and it is where the Blue Ball Syndrome reigns supreme over all mental and physical prisons of the heart as we all try to find our special one in our lives. I could see at this point of our conversation that Cynthia had begun to develop a few tears in her eyes and I could feel her pain.

I asked her, "Are you crying because Phillip is the way that he is or do you know that he is not faithful to you and you feel trapped in your fear of loneliness without him?"

Cynthia sat back in her chair and wiped her eyes and replied, "I hear his phone ring sometimes and it's not me calling him at night and sometimes on the weekends. I caught him kissing a girl one time but I forgave him and he promised not to be with her anymore. I feel foolish sometimes for taking him back and I feel he is cheating again on me and I hate myself for allowing him to get away with this."

At this point, the truth finally came out that Cynthia knew that Phillip was simply using her for sex but she was trapped by her own weakness and fears of being alone.

I was amazed at how such a beautiful girl could get caught up by someone like Phillip, but it is the heart of the woman that Phillip has and he knows it and he uses it to his advantage.   Women often do the same to men and sometimes are better at it than men are.

Cynthia in this case was a victim of Blue Ball Syndrome and feared being by herself and she was screaming out to me for help.

I only looked at her and said this one thing, "Cynthia, your worst fear has already happened to you, it has now become aware to you that you are living your worst fear already in your life and that is

Blue Ball Syndrome 33

you being alone, even when Phillip is in your presence."

Cynthia replied, "You know you are right, I guess that is why I am feeling so horrible every day and feeling worthless and like a door mat to Phillip."

I replied, "that's exactly why you feel the way you do Cynthia and right now Phillip has the power over you and you do not have the power of your life because you have turned your free will over to Phillip who is using you and your beautiful body for his satisfaction while leaving you unsatisfied and unfulfilled."

I continued, "You can take that power back if you would only see 31 years as a stepping stone and not a stumbling block, you can take the power back if you see your potential for opening your heart to someone not as a weakness but as courage to try new things and that includes new people as well. Lastly, Cynthia you can take the power from Phillip when you recognize that you are the star of your own life's play and he is nothing but a stage hand that can always be fired and replaced by an endless supply of applicants for the job. In the production of your life's play, you are the director, producer and star of your life's theatre, no one else should share that spotlight."

Cynthia laughed with joy in her voice and she replied, "You know, I have never heard anyone say anything so profound before and I will make my life's play work for me in my life starting today, I thank you for that great illustration of how to empower myself to control my life." Cynthia continued, "I know I have been wasting my time with Phillip, he is very selfish and does not satisfy me at all sexually, he is just a tease to what I want. I feel absolutely lonely whenever he is around and I hate that feeling of having a man and being withheld from satisfaction as a woman should, you know?"

I replied, "Yes Cynthia, I know all too well and that is why I can tell you that you are not alone, many men and women hate sexual teasers that perpetrate like they are God's gift to us all when it is usually the other way around. People who can truly love and are not selfish to themselves like you and me are God's gift to the world and especially to anyone who can love, appreciate and value the unique and wonderful persons we are."

I continued, "Naturally, this is the proper way to love what God can truly give a person. Phillip dominates or plays out his teasing of sexual gratification to you and never delivers on that promise to you. This is how men get frustrated with women as well who tease them with the illusion of sexual satisfaction but are merely users of good natured men. Ironically, Cynthia, I have been a victim too, but like you I took my power back and threw them skank bitches out of my life."

Cynthia and I laughed and continued our lunch, seeing her laugh and her knowing that she could take her power back from Phillip made lunch even better. I can truly see now why women as well as men hate sexual teasers.

Chapter 4

GOOD FELLAS, KEEPING THEIR WOMEN SATISFIED

Believe it or not, there is a population of good males out there that are not cheaters or "baby daddy" wannabe types of men. These men are not as uncommon as some women think.

I cannot for the life of me understand why some women feel that after a few knuckle headed experiences with some sorry men that all men follow that pattern.

It has been my experience that many women get into the mode that all they see relates to the whole world of what they know about their life. Consequently, these same women have never traveled outside of their home surroundings or even lived outside of what they have always known.

Most women that have explored college life or even visited other states or other major cities in the US or abroad all have a real sense of what different men are all about.

Men who are capable of loving a woman are not hard to find. They are all around and they are usually the men who do not make a lot of noise in the crowd. Men who are the "good fellas" in our society are usually sober minded in their activities, right in thought and possess a great sense of religious influence. These men are always looking for wisdom as to how to treat a woman and are usually groomed by older more relationship prosperous men on how to be a better man.

I was surprised to learn that in almost every church that men attend there is a men's ministry that is groomed by Deacons and Elders that help men see themselves in the Bible and help to council men and even their families.

I learned from my friend Dennis that the 100 Men Organization actually helps men to be better individuals with regards to who they are as well as mold the community that they serve to be better for the women and their families. This is a noble function in the African-American community that is needed in order to dispel the rumor that most men of African-American descent have non-positive attributes based on negative stereotypes.

Adversely, "hood style videos" and movies depicting "ghetto" themes demonstrating African-American men as pimps, hustlers and drug dealers are all most other races see of men of African descent.

Ironically, in years past, Hollywood was fixated on the African-American male image as low class and dark, not in skin color, but in morality and sinister thug like imagery that turned into huge profit sells for big budget studios. However, the "good fellas", as I call them, are always above Hollywood's imagery in our everyday reality.

In stark contrast, most African-American men are educated, married and faithful. Good men really do come home to their families and are actually involved in some form of familial relationship. This primary effect is totally opposite of what is seen in everyday music videos and depictions of African-American men as pimps and players.

In fact, before most African-American men enter into the industry of videos and Hollywood depicted imagery of what home life is actually like, many come from homes that are created from every day struggling families (some good homes and some broken) with an absent father and disconnected relationships.

This contributes to the hood effect where education is not important and money "is king". Being selfish and all about yourself is a common way of life for the everyday pimp, thug & hustler. Worst of all is the molester of youth that is included in this bunch due to the prison mentality that most of the Hollywood and music industry thrives on today.

Obviously, the molester is the shame and animal instinct of an untrained and uneducated man of any ethnicity. This is usually the thief with low pants (due to no strings allowed in pants from prison life). This person will kill for sport and commit the most heinous crimes anywhere from rape to mass murder of youth with little regard to the after effects it has on the life of the victims and family members left behind.

Consequently, it is almost like the victim of this man's anger was in his way even if they were innocently attending a party or minding their own business and had something that the molester wanted for his own selfish, lazy and uneducated animalistic concern. Unfortunately to report, this animal in human form is becoming very prevalent in our society and has now become a fixture in the hood, public schools and churches as well.

The one way you can sight this animal is to look out for many evident signs that demonstrate the character of this animal in human form. One way to identify this character is to see how it appears. Low pants where the underwear are showing, the conversation is filled with profanity and the substance is usually all about how good they have done many things that include nothing in substance of achievement as a claim to fame.

This individual is all about their sexual nature of satisfaction and usually approach women by saying, "what's up girl, let me get that good sex with you? I am good like that, I am not looking for any love, I just want some dome (oral sex) and some great penetration, what's up tonight?"

As you can see, this guy is all about himself and his nature. These guys love drinking and smoking and are usually out late at night. Their life is all about the criminal mentality. This person thrives on negative things and while even in prison will rape another man to satisfy his animal like nature, then he will come out of jail and have unprotected sex with a female just as easily as he had unprotected sex with a man in jail.

This is the animalistic nature of some men that will commit crimes that will cost others their lives or harm innocent ones by exposing them to any and everything from HIV, drugs and worst, death. Sadly to say, women are still falling for the nature of the Hollywood male in human form.

According to statistics released in 2007, many minorities are raised in single parent homes without the presence of a father figure. The effect of the absent male in the life of women can leave women without a model of a good man. Unfortunately, women are intrigued with that "bad boy syndrome" and often find him exciting. The woman's lack of her ability to discern a real man yields many women to be caught as prey caught in the spider's web when dealing with the animalistic male in our society.

This is what brings on many instances of early pregnancies, abortions, HIV and worst the emotional scars that are not seen but felt by many women in our community. Unfortunately, there are no medications or healing balms to help recover from the wounds of mistrust.

"Good Fellas", on the other hand, are the real fruit of the community. These are the morally built, well educated men that value their families and seek to build relationships filled with spiritual sensitivity that adheres to keeping the moral code of generations to come moving forward. Because of these "good fellas", hope still reigns supreme for women in our society while also providing the faith and endurance to maintain a sense of self preservation in hopes of attaining the right to be called the woman that stands beside this man of honor. Furthermore, these men actually outnumber their competition.

The men adorned with "good fella" standing separate what defines a successful, focused stable minded man from one that seeks to achieve his own personal goals and dreams, by any means necessary, without thinking twice about who may get hurt in the process.

If it were not for the "good fellas" we would not have advanced as far as we have in our society. If it were not for the good fellas then all male minority communities would not have progressed to their extent and would not have the positive impact that they currently have today.

Most minority communities have always embraced the concept of the "good fellas" and how to be better in society and come above the stereotypes that Hollywood and the music industry have portrayed about them.

Moreover, many women have the concept that good men are not around. Well that cliché is a myth that was started by women that made bad choices in their lives and got stuck in their bad choices that lead to poverty, depression and obesity.

They basically gave up on themselves due to past mistakes with the animalistic male that they fell in love with and unfortunately he left them with a bag of empty promises that included some kids and a life time of debt and disappointment. I can clearly see this specific type of woman saying that there are no good men around because of some choices that this particular female made in her life. Ironically, this female does not have to decide every female's future.

Consequently, there are still many good men around. Some of the women that I previously describe often times have no means to attract a man good caliber based on their inadequacies and lack of means to contribute to the success of not only this, but any relationship they are involved in. Men are just as guilty as women when it comes to not recognizing the gift of Proverbs Chapter 31 woman staring them in the face and failing to recognize her.

I mention this to let my female readers know that when a woman is educated (not only academically but also in life) and sober in thought and mind, she embodies all the attributes that describe that women in that chapter of Proverbs. For those that may not be familiar with that passage of scripture, that type of woman aligns her motives and actions for her own life with ultimately displaying characteristics of a great wife, friend and confidant.

Blue Ball Syndrome

Women who take the time to educate themselves in various ways and take care of their personal and familial responsibilities will often inspire other women to take care of themselves spiritually, educationally and physically.

The Proverbs Chapter 31 woman maintains herself while also completing her responsibilities to her God, her husband and her family. This is a unique character trait that any man that sees himself as part of the "good fellas" looks for in the woman he wishes to call his own.

The Book of Proverbs is a book of scripture in the Holy Bible that I often reference when I counsel men that are looking to a certain woman as a future potential lifemate. In my humble opinion, and also because of my personal beliefs, I am not a great judge of female characteristics.

However, the Holy Bible is a great roadmap that will guide any man as he begins to narrow his search for what to look for in a suitable female partner. Believe me, there are plenty of good Proverbs Chapter 31 females out there that are ripe and ready for marriage and children. These female companions will really love and faithfully devote themselves to a great man willing to share his life with her. I have met many of these women in my own personal travels.

Despite what is depicted on the movie screen, I'd argue that society as a whole does not believe that all minority females are easy, I say to society don't believe Hollywood in the sense that all minority females are viewed as rank sexual objects. This is not a true stereotype and could not be further from the truth. This is usually a European view of minority women that goes back historically to the days of slavery and domination of European slave masters from Portugal, Spain and America. Slave masters would rape the African slave women and perform all kinds of sex acts with them for pleasure and yet be married to the exclusive European female as a status symbol in society at that time.

This is yet the mentality that Hollywood ascribes to in our society that portrays minority females, especially African-American, Latino and Asian women as sex hungry, possessed vixens for all ethnicities to exploit. However, this is not true of all females of minority descent and most good men are not fooled by this depiction. Most minorities are not affected by these negative connotations that are repeatedly expressed in our society, on television, in the movies and in magazines.

In general, symptoms associated with Blue Ball Syndrome can be avoided when good men and sober minded females who possess a Proverbs Chapter 31 mentality unite and become the type of couple God desires for them to be. The Book of Proverbs also provides instructions for men as to how they were set amongst the Elders of the land and had achieved great income and sustenance for their families, they had respect and clout in their business dealings which were always done with fairness and stability of a sober mind, and also embraced a wife and family. A Proverbs Chapter 31 man does not look like Hollywood's thuggish animalistic portrayal of men that were previously mentioned in this chapter.

Rather, these men aim to become scholastically and worldly well-educated, well rounded and respectful men of integrity. These men lead their lives in a way that demonstrates the fear and admonition of God with a great sense of morality that attracts the Proverbs Chapter 31 woman.

All indications allude to the fact that these men aren't drinkers, smokers or revilers who have broken spirits and are filled with grief. This type of behavior is not common for "good fellas" with consideration to their personal and societal levels of influence.

Ultimately, "good fellas" and Proverbs Chapter 31 women are the types of individuals the Holy Bible deem as the best any generation has to offer with regards to finding an ideal mate. Both sexes, in this context desire the same thing, an ideal mate that wishes to be loved and to share in life's quest for the good and wonderment that love, sincerity and companionship have to offer.

Only good things can come from so many men and women attempting to pursue education and financial security to make better decisions and improve society and the integrity of the family.

From an African-American viewpoint, the election of President Barack Obama and his wife indicate that it is okay to be part of the "good fellas". By all accounts, the relationship we see between his wife Michelle and their daughters Sasha and Malia provides a look into what happens when a Proverbs Chapter 31 woman aligns herself with a likeminded man. No longer is it impossible to achieve this level of President Obama's achievement.

Regardless of whether or not our African-American men and women reach what can be deemed as the pinnacle of success by securing the Presidency of the United States, these individuals aspire to make good choices and move progress of mankind forward.

Chapter 5

WHY A HARLOT/CONCUBINE IS NOT A BAD THING FOR THE SEXES

This chapter touches on a sensitive subject matter and is written for the mature minded person who is willing to open their minds and receive what is being said, even if you disagree with the ultimate conclusions being drawn. This chapter was written in order to stimulate interest and encourage men and women to talk about what we do not customarily talk about in our churches, homes and institutions that deal with human nature.

This chapter is meant to inspire and show how people relate Blue Ball Syndrome in its most unique way possible as the human touch and sensual nature of love and passion becomes absent from the state of an existing relationship. Moreover, in many relationships, people are yet holding on to vows out of desperation yet the passion of the relationship has diminished to an all too familiar place in American society.

This type of relationship existence creates a disparity and isolates one in the marriage and diminishes that covenant bond to a casual relationship typical of a boyfriend and girlfriend. This isolation of the human emotion may create a smothering effect and leaves the heart alone and abandoned.

Generally, this is a terrible place to be while in a relationship and often influences many men and women to respond to these periods of abandonment in many different ways. This is where the nature of the response and its effect can often drive people to do things that in good times in their relationship would never be considered.

I have found in my research for this project that many women have found that the heart is a sacred vault filled with all the wonderful things that their man has done for them in times past such as places they've traveled together and romantic moments that were shared. Honestly, this is how many relationships build trust and love from one woman to one man; this is the nuts and bolts of most societal relationships.

Most of the female participants in my interviews were educated and financially well off. Some were married and a few were single, but my intent was to seek out those that were married to talk about this chapter. I wanted to convey a sensible understanding of some credible feedback on the subject of harlots and concubines in our society today.

Furthermore, I wanted to view the historical context of those women as it relates to today's view on relationships. The chapter will reveal how harlots and concubines have affected the households in present marriages and contributed to the ideology of divorce in today's society.

Blue Ball Syndrome

The results of my research were amazing (in my opinion) and I truly have a greater sense of what is happening in marriages across the country based on these interviews. As an isolated event, this experience really influenced me to write this chapter as honest and forthcoming as I possibly could.

Most of the men that I interviewed were married and a few were single (three were divorced). A total of 76 men and 68 females were interviewed for this chapter, including situations where marriages worked and others where marriages failed. The methods in which some people have chosen to keep their marriages together (in the oddest possible fashion) will cause many raised eyebrows while others would never even consider these tactics.

Uniquely, in most of the interviews, I talked with both men and women about the symptoms associated with Blue Ball Syndrome and their experiences with marriage and casual relationships. This has been a real pattern of how many people have devoted themselves toward remaining faithful in their relationships and yet have sought out sexual alternatives like a harlot or concubine to provide the sexual satisfaction portion of a marriage.

Most people remained married either for the sake of the children or because they really loved their spouses but did not like the abandonment of affection at times from the spouse. Moreover, this now brings us into the question, "is a harlot or a concubine a bad thing if you have a successful marriage or a great relationship?" According to many men that I interviewed (a good representation of all nationalities), it was not so alarming that many of them told me that they would never cheat on their spouses or abandon them knowingly in their relationships or marriages.

However, when the question was posed, "if you felt abandoned in your relationship or marriage would you consider a female companion like a harlot or concubine that was not your girlfriend or spouse?", unanimously, the answer was yes! 86% of the men responded that they would consider a harlot or a concubine in these situations.

Men felt that due to the stress that a wife or girlfriend could inflict on him (in that situation) he could become frustrated while in love at the same time with his wife or girlfriend.

Ironically, women were posed with a similar question, "If you felt abandoned in your relationship or marriage would you consider a male companion like a harlot or concubine that was not your boyfriend or husband that would cater to your most intimate needs?" 68% of the females responded yes, however 32% said no. The women, who responded no, would try to work it out with their spouses or boyfriends and mentioned that having a relationship is a good thing even in bad times. The 68% of females and the 86% of men are the target population of my study because they were for the most part people who were married for 5 years or more and many had children.

Blue Ball Syndrome

This information was also broken down by age groups where most men I interviewed fell in age ranges from 26 to 62. The females' ages ranged from ages 25 to 59. Many of the participants had been married for over 5 years and the oldest marriage was over 20 years in length.

It also seemed that the older the marriage, the more the two people had to endure and had accepted of each other. I had found out that many men had already had experiences outside of their marriages. Most men had not told their spouses due to the fact that most had replied that they actually really still deeply loved their spouses.

It seems that men are lovers of their spouses but can have unemotional sex for simple satisfaction without the emotional attachments that they already have established in their marriages. The males I interviewed all emphasized having protected sex as well thinking about their spouses even when they were with someone else. Most men expressed that they did not abandon the marriage because their heart was still with their spouse and family.

It seems that sexual gratification and the feeling of having a fantasy fulfilled with someone other than the married men or women at home was not as exciting as having sex with a harlot or concubine. It also seems that most of the 86% of the male responders agreed that a harlot or concubine was soothing to the male personality and they catered to the men making them feel special and very sexy as a man, this really made their male potential as a sexual conqueror come to life once again.

In many male responders case, the harlot gave them the uplift for their own male self-esteem and gratification of being with someone that provided a non-confrontational intimate experience. Men were relaxed and were made to feel special by the harlot; this was a real turn-on for many of the male responders.

In contrast, the females included in the 68% stated they had considered a harlot and a few of them had previously had an affair; two of the female responders actually had a man on the side that has been around for quite some time.

It seems that women are more emotional seekers and open themselves up to an affair with a man based on the aspect of emotional abandonment that the husband has not provided them in the marriage. Most of the female responders made an emphasis that their husbands do not see them as he once did and this increased the quest for women to seek that gratification outside of the marriage itself.

Of the 68% of women, 27 of them had children and also stated they wouldn't allow their man on the side to meet their children.

All of the females agreed that they would never tell their spouses of their sexual affairs. It seems that women and men have one thing in common when it comes to Blue Ball Syndrome and that is when the physical and emotional gratification of the spouse goes missing in the marriage or relation-

Blue Ball Syndrome

ship, the pain of abandonment is so heart felt that most of the responders reported that there is a void like an empty space. Only another's human touch with a sexual, pleasurable experience would fill the void. It also sheds a unique light on how marriage or relationships can be viewed with the use of a harlot or concubine in lieu of having these emotions and voids filled by a spouse or a mate. Harlots and concubines were a tool that leveled anger and even provided the fantasy of satisfaction without emotional attachment that did not feel like cheating to the responders in my study.

Ironically, with men and women, a harlot or concubine can be quite soothing to the psychological stress of the disappointment that can be often caused by a spouse. Even the most loveable and trusting spouse can cause undeniable pain with harsh words uttered that can push a spouse into the awaiting comforting and often soothing arms of a harlot/concubine.

Harlots/Concubines can be either male or female to the opposite sex and occasionally, even the same sex. I was a little surprised that there are male harlots/concubines just as there were females that were providing these services as well.

It seems that women and men were willing to pay for sexual gratification due to the fact that the responders of the study did not have to feel dedicated to this individual. This kept them free of the drama of getting into a love triangle situation where it would come back and be found out by the spouse or significant other.

It seems that many of the female and male responders had been honest about their sexual orientation and enjoyed sexual interludes with the opposite sex. However, 7 of the female responders admitted that they had been with a female before and 3 had an open mind to sex with females and not always exclusively preferred male harlots/concubines when seeking outside physical sexual gratification.

What really amazed me in my research was that many of the responders, male and females alike, mentioned that they had all been married for over 5 years, the longest married person I interviewed had been married for 20 years and had experienced a harlot/concubine and actually enjoyed the experience, he stated that he actually appreciated his wife more after he had his time with the harlot/concubine as it demonstrated to him that the harlot/concubine was more for social interaction and sexual satisfaction.

The responder thought this was good and enjoyed the way the harlot treated him and made him feel special with great sex acts and a great massage that he loved that he did not get at home with his wife of 20 years.

Quite naturally, prostitution is the oldest known profession in the history of recorded working men and women and is practiced all over the world.

Blue Ball Syndrome

In fact, in some countries prostitution is actually legal. It seems that in certain countries there are designated areas for prostitution to be practiced that liberates the areas from crime and public pollution of women stalking men and infiltrating tourists in main parts of the city of the countries that allow prostitution.

Most countries that allow prostitution recommend females and males to have HIV tests and the profession is taxed to afford these types of preventive services. There are designated areas where the women and men provide their services. These areas are very well respected and all abide by the local government regulation of the areas.

Nevada is the only state in the continental United States that legally allows prostitution to be practiced. Ranches full of women are located on the outskirts of town and for a fee, many of the women pleasure both men and women who want that special type of catering that provides sexual satisfaction.

It seems that in these free designated areas the town provides free health screenings for the working ladies and often some of the work facilities actually provide room and board for the women working in the clubs and bars that allow legal prostitution.

As I began to look up countries and even legal prostitution in the state of Nevada in the United States, I began to wonder if the US would allow prostitution to be a legal working occupation. I wondered how that would benefit the local government and possibly even the economy. As I performed my research on the Internet, prostitution is reportedly a billion dollar business worldwide and practiced in America and all countries of the world.

Each night, all over the world, prostitution is practiced by women and men who hire themselves out to the highest bidder who will pay the fee for great sexual gratification and soothing moments of psychological and physical pleasuring that both will equally enjoy.

Legalizing prostitution will provide the financial reimbursement various cities need to implement a health prevention program that would dramatically reduce the spread of HIV and would this require all legal working women and men who profit from the profession to obtain a monthly HIV test and physical exam.

This would help monitor the spread of HIV and also help to promote prevention of the spread of HIV among communities by allowing treatment programs and clinics that would be designated for the preventive health of sexual transmitted diseases.

Taxation of the prostitution industry enforced by the government prevents raising taxes on the local citizens or adversely interfering with the local economy. This could be a win-win situation by providing cleaner city districts and streets and a reduction of sexual transmitted diseases with better preventive programs that would limit how HIV/STD are spread amongst the prostitution industry.

This legalization would designate prostitution in certain areas of the city or state away from residential homes, business and tourist districts. This would allow cleaner street corners and better monitoring of drug use and drug trafficking in areas where crime and prostitution normally flourish while actually maintaining and securing these areas to cut down on the influx of drugs and the associated violence on women as well.

One of the male participants of my study stated that he had been to Amsterdam and visited the Red Light District where both prostitution and marijuana (in small quantities) is legal and may be purchased on the street.

Ironically, the rate of HIV in countries where prostitution is legal is lower by almost 40% in comparison to the United States.

Also, the drug problems that currently exist in the United States is not even close to being a problem in Amsterdam. There are very few drug problems in Amsterdam and many of the locals do not smoke marijuana even though it is so abundantly available.

It seems that legalizing prostitution and marijuana has taken the taboo out of the social ills and has made it a taxable and profitable trade that benefits the local society and city of Amsterdam where all citizens profit equally.

Returning to the chapter topic, we must look at the harlot as an individual and get their point of view on this very controversial subject matter. I did not find any male harlots to interview but I did find one female harlot on the internet to interview, her given name is Sasha. I was amazed at what she said about men and women in the prostitution industry and how she felt about it all.

I was personally curious as to how Sasha got started in the industry. Her answers were very straight forward and brutally honest. For the sake of confidentiality, no last name was revealed nor the place where Sasha provided services.

This is our interview in her own words.

Q: "So Sasha, tell me, how did you get started in the escort business?"

A: "I was first introduced to the business at a bachelor party and the guys were very much into my body and they wanted to get a little freaky. So, I took off my shirt and allowed the groom-to-be to feel my breasts and have a great time with me. I performed oral sex on him and the guys went wild and I had a good time just seeing that I could please a man and get paid good money, it was great!"

Q: "Who are your main clients that you see often?"

Blue Ball Syndrome

A: "I mainly see professional males that are your average executive types and men who are well to do and sport figures and some professional athletes and business executives that like to take trips to come and see me. A few actually send me a plane ticket to come where they are. Most of my clients are married and many have kids and nice well to do families. I mean the men I spend my time with will have to do well [financially] because they have to pay my fee for my great services I give them."

Q: "Sasha, how much do you charge for your services?"

A: "I usually charge a rate of $500.00 per hour and that rate has fluctuated as high as $550.00 per hour for a new client or someone I do not know or wants more services than I normally offer."

Q: "Sasha, why do you think most married men experience Blue Ball Syndrome at home and seek your services?"

A: "Well, I have talked to many married men over my time in this business and it seems that the trophy wife they married is not the lasting woman they thought she would be. Most of my married men complain to me that she does not want have sex the way the man wants it. You know, most guys like good soothing missionary position sex with the legs up and out so that the man can get into his woman. Well a lot of women who are married do no keep that up with their men.

Men also like getting that pussy from the back and feeling the masculine dominance over a female or their wives. But for some strange reason, some women either lose interest or they lose their effect on the man and do not keep up with the man's desires that all married men have, especially if they are under cover freaks that have a great sex drive and still like to have a great sexual encounter with his women almost like a date."

Q: "Sasha what do most men like for you to provide for them and how do you make a man forget his wife?"

A: "Well, that is easy because once a man starts looking outside the house he rarely wants to find love and a new headache to deal with. Shit, most guys are looking for some stress relief and some good head which is a blow job let me be real about that! Men love to have their dick sucked and the balls licked. Not many wives suck dick after so many years of marriage and that is crazy. I make it my business to suck my man's dick everyday and make his ass cum like he is a diamond star of the mother fucking Dallas cowboys for real! That is why most married guys get blue balls or lonely at home because they are unhappy with someone that does not cater to those intimate men like fantasies anymore.

Man, this is where I step in and they pay me for what the damn wife won't do. I mean, I am not a home wrecker or some shit. The tricks come to me and ask me for my services and pay me well for what I do. I am the fantasy that they wish they had at home! For the most part, most men would love to have a harlot for a wife and a trophy woman with good brains who was smart and pretty and had the book knowledge like a lawyer or doctor all in one. But not every man obviously can find that package."

Q: "Do you think Prostitution should be legalized?"

A: "Wow, with the rate of how people fuck and have all kinds of affairs around, you would think that it was already legal man! Hell, you would think that the damn banks stealing tax payer's money from out of hard working people's pockets would be a crime but that shit is legal as hell and you know that is a mother fucking crime all day long!

Man, I don't know why the law would lock our asses up for doing something with our own bodies usually in our own private places for some money that a man is willing to pay for? I mean I am not robbing a man, I am providing a damn service to the community and truth be known, I am actually providing more psychological services to men than society thinks. I am the one men run to when there are problems at home with the wife. I am the one most men chose when the job is hard and they want some power back from the boss and want their manhood restored and don't want no crap or back talk from the wife of how the day was or don't want a mother fucker to get on their nerves.

All my clients know, I am going to sooth them with a good massage because I am a massage therapist by day. I am going to go all out to pamper them and suck that dick until he cums in my mouth. I always use a condom but, I don't stop oral sex until my client cums in my mouth then I know he feels good and all my clients loves me for that because they don't even feel the condom in my mouth. I lay down missionary style or doggy style and allow my clients to relieve his stress by letting them fuck that pain out and restore them back to how they should feel, and then they go home to the wife after my therapy session for real!

Shit, I am the one that gives men the uncompromising comfort in providing council for them by allowing the man to feel my warm mouth and my tongue stroking them and it is massaging the day's pain and anxiety away from them. Man, all my clients tell me they need that and they are all married. I actually encourage and tell my clients to

Blue Ball Syndrome

go home to the wife and try to work it out because I know I am not trying to love nobody! But, I provide that service and quite frankly women have been providing it since the beginning of fucking time so why make what the hell I do some secret or immoral thing when most things done on Wall Street and in Washington D.C. should be immoral too."

Q: "Alright Sasha, what do you think about harlots on the street corner doing their thing; is that something that you support?"

A: "Now that shit is usually why good women in this business get a bad name. Those tricks are out there usually due to a pimp or some trick that's done turned them into some form of a crack head and the bitch got to find some way to afford her drugs or the pimp's money and his drugs too and that is a damn shame! That is what fucks it up for most good women like myself who own my shit and I have never been on some corner, hell no. I have too many men first of all that respect my profession and treat me like they would a Lawyer or a Doctor. I am considered a high profile escort and many guys would love to be in my client. I have long brunette hair, beautiful skin, natural hazel green eyes, 34-22-34 is my figure and it is hot.

I work out 3 times a week; I have my own apartment for my clients and they like that. I have my own massage business but I don't get down like that at work. I do often visit with my clients at their offices or some private location so it is never an on the street kind of encounter. I dress casual and stylish with class because I am a woman with class. All my clients like to hang with me.

In fact, one is taking me to Oakland, CA this weekend just so he can have some company on his business trip so that is the kind of men, I deal with. Now, does that sound like a corner harlot to you? Hell no, it sounds like a woman that is doing what she can do to keep it real and have a career and make some money on the side with providing a service to men who just want to be pampered and respected and not have a bitch get on their nerves!

It's the low class corner whore that keeps the profession illegal because people associate this profession with drugs, crime, murder and domestic violence but that could not be further from the truth. The truth is, when you allow yourself to be used and beaten and don't know your worth that's when the pimps on the streets take over and those women. They get strung out on the street drugs which is crack or ecstasy and crazy shit like meth-amphetamine. Hell, that's what the public sees quite often and most importantly it is what scares so many in societies of certain cultures of the street life. Let me make this point also, that many of the street whores are not very attractive or classy in there dress. Of course, not even you would be

Blue Ball Syndrome

interested in a lady hanging all there, shit out for all to see without some class and style about yourself, damn! Even a trick want a woman to look half way decent man!

I mean if you saw me on the street you would not know if I was a lawyer or a professional business person or an executive going to work. I look like a professional well to do white woman all the time and that's how I attract my clients. Street whores have no class and so they have no choice but to let the street eat that ass up and that is where HIV and contaminated drug needles and all that bad shit came from man, believe me. Most of those girls are just neglected out there by a society that the pimp and the streets take full advantage often the simple bitches and use their ass.

I feel for them, because after that life with the pimps and the street drugs, most women lose their teeth. Some of them look rough man with no style or class and many of them are not naturally attractive after that hard life on the street corners. What's worst is [that] most have a criminal record and they are not respected for what they do and that is always a terrible reality at the end of the day for selling your ass to men for money trying to please a pimp!"

Q: "Do you use a pimp since you have been in this business?"

A: "No way man, I have never used a pimp; I did not need to. I am a very attractive, mixed of heritage white woman and all men love how I look. I have long natural brunette hair past my shoulders when it is down, and great skin completion no scars or sores or blemishes on my skin, no crazy marking on my body. I eat right and I take care of my health, I work out and watch my money and my spending in this recession. I have my own massage business and I own my own place. Now with all that being said do you really think I need a damn pimp? Man, those pimps are the mother fuckers that get the bitches killed and hurt on them damn drugs and usually are the real perpetrators on the streets that rob those dumb broads of their class, money, looks and esteem.

It has got to be hard living like that so I never entertained that lifestyle, I have always represented myself and I have always been high class with my shit! That's why I earn $500.00/hour just like some lawyers do because I give a great service just like they do and I am the best at what I do so I deserve to receive a good reward for my services. Anyways, a pimp does not have the damn brain power I have to even advertise the whores right on the street! That lets you know right there a damn pimp ain't shit! So I have never used them nor do I care to use them because most of their asses are broke felons that deal drugs with criminal records that are just loafing off of low class level bitches on the street that got caught up in the game man, that's the real

Blue Ball Syndrome

truth on that and I feel I told you the real deal right there!"

Q: "How do you set the mood for the man who is looking for a night out that may have symptoms of Blue Ball Syndrome?"

A: "Well, usually the men will contact me on the internet or by my private phone that I keep for guys who are referred to me by other clients that I trust. I can tell when a man is lonely or just wants to have some company or is just lusting for some ass. I always ask the man what he wants because that is the key. When you find out what a man wants then how to please him is simply listening to his desires and laying out that scenery for that individual becomes quite easy. When I first meet a new client, I try to put him at ease by talking to him finding out why he wants to be with me and what he wants to do. Once I know that then I have the man undress and I help him undress, I want him to feel that I care and enjoy him by providing intimacy and comfort. I like providing my client's with a nice massage, a sensual whole body massage that ultimately relaxes my client. You can tell that the man is relaxed because you can hear that hmmm... sound, you know. That is the sound that the days stress is slowly going away from the man. After the massage, I have the man either lay down on my bed of satin sheets, clean and fresh with candles already lit for romantic effects.

If he prefers I then like to submit to the man's desires and get on my knees with a soft pillow under my knees in front of the man. Men like my hair down and I take his dick which is usually rock hard by now and will gently kiss him from his lips to his dick, I cleverly place my condom in my mouth which my clients never know or sometimes can't even feel and I began to perform oral sex on him. I love pleasing a man in this format because men love for a woman to totally give them a fantasy and most beautiful women can get anything from a man if she would only get on her knees and suck his dick with passion, all men love it and they ask for it. I love doing it and I do it so that my man can relax and release his anxiety of his frustrations right there in my mouth and I can feel my client as I massage that dick with my warm tongue very gently but firmly preparing him to cum! I know when he looks down into my eyes while I am on my knees with his dick in my mouth that he is enjoying it. It makes my client realize that he is the king again and he still has his manhood that society did not steal his years of youth from him.

Most importantly, right now he is living a fantasy with a lovely beautiful white woman with long hair, lovely skin soothing his dick in her mouth all down my throat. I am not stopping until he cums in my mouth as I massage the man's balls and gently but firmly suck the entire length of his dick, men love that. Then there it is, boom!... The ejaculation

Blue Ball Syndrome

happens and he thinks I am done and I am not! I keep sucking and massaging his balls even more because men are very sensitive in the head of the penis when they cum, so I massage the head and use my hand to massage his balls at the same time and all men love it and I know he is in heaven on earth and he feels empowered by me and I have put him back on top of his world again. From this point on, many men will tell me that they either want to get into my pussy or just talk."

Either way, I am cool with it. So, I usually just lay beside the man and massage his dick and rub him sensually with some nice oils and either we talk about his day or he has intimate sex with me and puts a condom on and performs good missionary style sex first. Men, love to feel a woman from her inside first and missionary style gives them that view of a woman's face and breast her passion for attraction for her man, it is a woman in her submissive warm sensual position where she can kiss and console a man at the same time.

My client's love missionary style because I wrap my legs around them and bring them into my pussy better and open up even deeper for them. I like it because it lets me control the man's thrust in me and not tear me up but it also allows me to feel close to my client and provide a romantic fantasy for him as he enjoys his experience even better. If my client desires, I turn over on my stomach and give him face down with my ass up position and men love this position as well especially some of my control freak clients! It lets them have control of my body and feel the animal nature of man over woman in a dominating role and this position is pleasing to me also because it allows me to give him power over a simple situation and men want and need that power from a woman."

When my client cums or ejaculates from these positions he is now on cloud nine. He is tired and excited and his level of satisfaction is at its peak, he feels empowered and is ready to go for another day. It is at this point, that we talk and I basically play counselor for my clients and soothe them with my words and my body massage and just kiss them gently as I lay with them. All men love it when a woman lies with them and caresses them. Men turn into babies at this point. If you noticed I never said anything about money because my clients already know he has to pay for my services but, I please him first and my pay has never been a struggle for any of my clients and you can see why."

Q: "Are all your clients white males or do you see other nationalities as well?"

A: "I see predominately all White married men for the most part but I have seen some African-American males as well. I have seen a few Asian men and some Latino men as well, so I would say I have seen a diverse group of men. White males like me because I am professional and discrete. My service is confidential and they want to pay for a

Blue Ball Syndrome

fantasy from me. African-American males that I have seen like the fantasy of White women like me submitting to them and making them feel special as a man and allowing that to happen for them gives me pleasure. I would say that about all my non-white clients as well. All of my clients are usually well to do and network my services amongst each other like a good fraternity secret or something. But, I like all men who can treat me with respect for what I do and respect me as a woman that wants to please the man and loves it. I really do love pleasing my client because I actually love sex. My thing is if a woman is going to do it, she better enjoy it and not be there for the money only because men know that game too and they hate it! I hear men talk about other broads to me and it is not good shit, believe me!"

Q: "Sasha, what is your advice for a woman that is struggling to keep her man from experiencing Blue Ball Syndrome?"

A: "That is too easy for me to answer. Most of my girlfriends do not know what I do on the side so I tell them what I do for my clients to please them. They will come back and say damn that shit worked; how the hell did you learn that and my response is well, it worked for thousands of years I just tapped into my male pleasing side of things. My girls are like what, you are on it girl. All a woman has to do is learn whatever her man wants and give that shit to him. It is so simple; if he wants his dick sucked, then do it. If he likes to see you in heels during sex then do it. If the man wants you to swallow and that is your husband then, damn it, do it! Men are like babies when it comes to sex because women are the milk and if a woman is not a great milk provider for her man, then her man continues to cry and long for that good shit, like me. I am going to give it to him because I love it and I am going to please him because I know I can.

I will send him back to his woman but he will always want to come back to his momma for some good milk, like mine. I know that might not sound righteous but shit, it is true. If women would not fight so much with their men and get on their damn nerves so much due to insecurity which can go both ways then their men would stay at home more. If women can learn how to submit to the man and provide him with a reason to stay home, that changes his mentality as well toward being at home with his wife or girlfriend. For example, provide a good home cooked meal, a nice massage for him; naturally, all men love a woman to perform oral sex on them. Get on your knees sometime and lay with him and just go all out to please him. I promise you, your man will be at home waiting on your ass hand and foot at night and he will not go anywhere, for real!"

Blue Ball Syndrome

Q: "We have talked about how the women could please their men but what do you think men can do to please the women out there who need attention as well?"

A: "That is really easy especially if a woman loves her man because most women just want their men to listen to them and cater to their needs that they may have. I have found that many women are really anxious for the man's affection and I am like that with my man. I crave my man's touch even though I do what I do. I still long for my man's presence and I want him to receive me body and soul and appreciate those sweet things that I try to do for him.

I mean, I cook and take care of my man even though I live my lifestyle on the side; I still like to prepare a meal for my man and I like going to the movies with him and I love dancing; my man is a protector so he loves opening doors for me and taking me out with him and I love it. I think men should take women out more and get her some typical things like a card every now and then just to let her know you care for her even if it is not her birthday of Mother's Day.

Men could really win over a good woman just really by doing what I do in my business and that is just laying out the simple things for the woman. For example, kiss her every day in the morning before you go off to work. Man that kiss may be simple but it will stay on your woman's mind all day and she will love you for something like that. Men usually should not forget her special plans like an event that she is planning or a special date she is excited about. A man must get into his woman and feel what she is feeling sometimes. It is true what they say, that men are more physical and women are much more emotional and intimate usually than a man is and that is my advice for men on their women."

Q: "I know you have lots of sex but what does your man do that is better than your other men that you deal with?

A: "My man treats me nice and he listens to me; he is totally my friend and he is open with me and makes me feel safe. I know with my clients, it is a performance but with my man I know he is with me because he cares for me from his soul. What he provides me with is what I wish all women had and that is someone who does not judge them or ridicule them for how they may feel about their lives or situations in their lives.

I have found that with my man that he is always there for me and I know after a day with my clients, that I can come home to love, peace and happiness. Many of my girlfriends wish they had something like I have but they are yet trying to find a man that is worth a damn without all the drama or deception that comes with the average stupid ass man that

Blue Ball Syndrome

does not really want to be serious in a stable relationship.

I know I am in the male catering business of providing pleasure but most couples really could keep their love life satisfied so much better at home if they only listened to each other's needs and wants more than when they want something or money."

Q: I know we talked about how you sexually please men, but how does a man sexually please his woman?"

A: "Wow, you are the first man that has ever asked me that question and I have talked to many men on this subject and that is really a great question. Men have to ask women what they like and men just assume what the woman may like from porno films or their boys and that is so off from the average woman. Most women, like a good fuck every now and then don't get me wrong, but if you don't ask you will not know what she wants or even how to please her.

I know a lot of my girlfriends like a man to perform oral sex on them but, I know quite a few who do not like it all the time or not at all. Some women are very sexually open like I and I love when my man taste my pussy but not all women are like me. Some women are very conservative and they need a man to really help them relax and they want the assurance that the sexual encounter and the opening of their heart will not to lead to a heart break in the future.

You have to understand that many women already have anxiety issues with men dogging them and playing around and not being serious with them. By the time she does meet a good guy, the typical woman, has already had at least three to four men in her life and all of them have left an impression on her. So the next man, if he is any good or caring will begin to help the woman heal and show her a different side then the typical selfish ass crazy mother fuckers that she met before the next potential man comes along. So men can be a great emotional strength to a woman if the man allows himself to really get to know his woman psychologically.

As far as sex is concerned, men must take their time and not be so in a hurry with their women. I have found that most of my girl friends complain about sex with their men because he is all about his ejaculation and excitement and cares less about her needs and that is not cool at all (if a man is going to keep his woman satisfied in bed)!

Men should provide massages to their women and rub their feet and touch her gently with some foreplay and always kiss her breasts gently and with ease (the nipples too, damn)! I mean some men act like they have to be forceful to be romantic and that is not the case at all. Men should caress the woman with a warm bath and hold her with his body and allow his masculinity to express passion

Blue Ball Syndrome

to the woman by performing oral sex on her. Men must really take the time with kissing and letting her know that the g-spot is not just a saying but a real place that you are trying to get her to arrive at her orgasm with your stimulation and all women love this pampering thing, believe me!"

Q: "Sasha, I thank you for your time and answering my questions as well as you have. I feel I have learned so much from this interview with you, any last words."

A: "Yes, tell the men out there to cook a home cooked meal every now and then. Women love going out but it is the effort of a man trying to please me by cooking a candle light dinner that is top notch to most women. It is said, the way to a man is through his stomach. Well, the same applies to a woman too. All women love this, trust me.

My man is not a chef, but he tries and I thank him every time because I love the way that he tries to please me. That's how he got me Doc; he cooked me dinner and I had never had a man cook for me before. I was hooked! So I turned him by doing what I do, but without the condoms as I got to know him better....oh, I loved it!

So we are just two people that blew each other's minds everyday...I simply love it!" I want my copy of this book doc, I wish you all the best; let me know if you need my services......bye Doc,"

I must admit, I was surprised and impressed with Sasha, I was not expecting such a stimulating exchange of ideas of collective thoughts from a professional harlot's point of view.

I felt that Sasha was a warm and easy person to speak with. I could certainly understand how she made so many people feel comfortable in her presence with the services that she provided. However, I began to think about the whole profession of prostitution, being considered a harlot and the history that harlots have had in historical times. Kings throughout the world have always had a harlot for comfort and sexual stress relief.

In fact, in ancient Egypt, it was customary for Kings and Pharaohs to have a harem of concubines and harlots that served the King or Pharaoh solely for his sexual pleasure. According to the bible, some women were raised in order to be sexual servants to the Pharaoh; it was considered an honor to be a harlot/concubine to the Pharaoh.

During the great life of King Solomon itself, as written in the book of (I) Kings, it is said that he had 700 wives and 300 concubines (I Kings 11:1-3) that served him. Even, the Queen of Sheba, (not a harlot) herself traveled from ancient Ethiopia, to the temple of the King Solomon across the Ethiopian desert to experience his wisdom and prosperity (I Kings 10:1-13). Therefore, the very history of prostitution really does have a unique place in the history of mankind.

This new revelation of harlots (even in the Bible) was a unique, eye opening experience even for me. I began asking myself, "what has the harlot done to improve society from ancient times until today from a historical perspective?"

Ironically, I had to once again go to the most ancient civilization recorded on earth that we still have a valid record on and that is the Holy Bible's record of the Egyptians and many descendants of the children of Israel in biblical times. It is recorded that there is a very famous harlot in the Old Testament by the name of Rahab. (Joshua 2:1 & 2:2-5).

Rahab was a famous harlot that spared the spies of the children of Israel from death. The army of Jericho searched for them to kill them and defeat the armies of Joseph, the leader of Israel after Moses died. Rahab is credited as a hero to the children of Israel and throughout the book of Joshua in the Bible. It is also noted that Rahab and all her family actually went to live with the army of the children of Israel after the great fall of the Jericho walls for her efforts to protect the spies of Israel. (Joshua 6:20-25).

Rahab is noted in the history of the Bible to have been married to an Israelite named Salmon who was a very affluent man. Rahab is actually the maternal ancestry of the likes of King David, King Solomon and even to Jesus Christ himself (Matthew 1:1-6). It is amazing how a harlot can be a hero throughout the Bible itself and provide an ancestral legacy to the Lord of Lord's and Kings of Kings Jesus Christ himself! Rahab's story is an amazing story of how a harlot that had good in her heart and became a wife to a very well educated prosperous man changed his life and became one of the most famous great grandmothers' in the history of the world!

Rahab is genetically linked to some of the greatest men ever to be recorded in the history of mankind. Historically, she was a Canaanite from the descendants of the Cushite nations, the original inhabitants of the land of Canaan. Today, this is modern day Turkey and parts of Southern Ethiopia and Egypt, reaching across modern day Palestine as well.

With this great history, one can only conclude that there is a real rich history of harlots in mankind's existence. It can be proved that there are some great things that can come from the life of a harlot. It is evident that a harlot, in the right circumstances of a loving man, can be a receiver of great intimacy and optimal satisfaction of her man and can have a positive effect on some of history's most influential men. A woman practicing the most uncommon of professions can positively influence Kings and Pharaohs despite being considered a harlot.

So I ask again, "Is there anything wrong with a harlot/concubine for the sexes?

Chapter 6

HAVE YOU LOOKED AT THE AVERAGE GUY?

The "average guy" is often described as the person that you see on the bus, at school, possibly at the book store or in the library. In the past, women have asked me, "Dr. Bell, do you feel like I will ever meet the right one in the crowd of people in my city?"

My response is always the same and that is, "you never know who you will meet until you look at the average guy or open your mind to what you see in the common places that you visit all the time."

For example, if you ever go to a place you frequently visit and see a nice looking guy but you never introduce yourself, you cannot blame anyone that you did not make a connection but yourself.

Many of us want to blame other people for a lack of friends and a lack of loved ones in our lives. The real truth is that we have not given ourselves enough opportunity to meet someone. It is so important to have an open mind when searching for a great companion.

We tend to look over the "average" people in our lives because the illusion created in the media (via music videos and what we see on television and in the movies) distorts what the heart usually sees.

The attraction between a man and a woman has always been obvious and in the truest sense of the word, it is defined by something as simple as a touch or a smile. It could possibly be an embrace that turns the heart into a great canvas of possibilities. "Average" people appear "run of the mill" on the outside. This type of man may have a little extra weight in his mid-section and not be as popular as other men.

The average guy may not articulate the best lines in the world to a man or woman or could be a little bit more conservative than the outgoing types. The difference is this person has not found the right person that he trusts to really understand his unique character other than beyond the outer shell that the world sees.

An average guy is not one that will judge you or make you feel inferior in your thoughts. The average guy may not dress in all the latest fashions. The average guy will not have all the answers that many will need to hear. But, in their defense, the average guy will have a laugh and a look that will be reserved for only you on the brightest or darkest of days.

Not many people look for average people anymore when searching for a mate. In my opinion, this is a real mistake. Life and love will never find you until you lose your fear of rejection. I am amazed at how afraid we are of someone telling us "no". In my opinion, "no", is what you allow it to be.

Blue Ball Syndrome

If you let the word 'no' become your prison, then you have already locked yourself out of life's lovely pleasures. Take a risk, turn the key and unlock your prison.

The fear of someone rejecting you can lead to self inflicted symptoms of Blue Ball Syndrome. The thought of this temporary humiliation of not having someone should never stop you from attempting to achieve your personal dreams in life. If you give a person more influence than a person should have (in your life), you have robbed yourself of the potential and strong possibility of a great date or great conversation.

A person's inability to overcome these types of battles may be seen as a weakness. In most cases, the average guy is waiting on you to overcome your fears and let your intentions be made known. Most importantly, if someone shows interest in you, it's alright to show interest in them.

Do not allow your mind to cause you to "chicken out" of a potentially great connection or worst, become afraid of what life could be trying to offer you. If the pursuer is not the type of person you are typically attracted to, at least be nice and greet them in a nice manner, even if the person is not the ideal person for you.

I would encourage the readers of this book to allow themselves room to relax and try new things such as dancing to have some fun when pursuing the average people

No one likes a wallflower. Not only that, no one likes an emotionally out-of-control sexual dynamo; therefore, you have to achieve some sense of balance in order to fully enjoy yourself.

Average people may wear glasses or contact lenses, but will only have eyes for you. They are able to hold a conversation about almost anything that truly interests you. This person will be able to relate to you at the grocery store, library, school house, college dorm and even the movie theatre. This person is a real powerhouse to embrace because of their unique appeal for love and life. At the end of the day, this is what both sexes desires anyway, a person after their own heart.

Being "average" can describe both males and females; they are whoever you need that person to be in order to satisfy your personal needs. My personal advice however, is not to be afraid to find someone considered "average"; the average guy may not have a certain hairstyle you like; he or she may have a natural stylish afro, wavy or curly hair or even dread locks.

The average guy may have long stringy blonde hair or red hair or maybe even be a brunette. The average guy can be of any ethnicity. If the average guy feels you as an individual and keeps you from experiencing Blue Ball Syndrome, then that person is the person for you. My hope is that each of you reading this will experience love and peace as you meet your ideal mate.

Blue Ball Syndrome

Hopefully, you will find someone you share common ground with, is fun loving and approachable. Always remember to never fear rejection. "No" is only the opportunity for someone else to say "yes"!

Chapter 7

LOOKING FOR LOVE VERSUS DESPERATE FOR SEX

I am sure that everyone has been lonely at some point in their lives. I recall that at some of my lonely moments, I sought out sex rather than seek love from another person. I sometimes thought that if a girl had sex with me, it would fill that internal void I had to experience love.

Ultimately, I realized I was always wrong but never could quite understand why. At this defining moment in my life, I was confusing desperate for sex for my quest for love. This occurred mostly in my early twenties, I did not think about love in the unique sense of the word, I only looked at the apparent (and instant) gratification for sexual pleasure as my connection for love at the time.

Love for me was a beautiful girl making love to me and just loving the feeling and going about my business after the fact with no strings attached. This was fun when I was younger but I never wanted to hurt anyone based on my mindset at the time.

I always tried to treat women right even though I was enjoying engaging in casual sex. It appeared that I would grade a girl by the way she performed sexually. If she was good and allowed me to do all the things I enjoyed doing to her, I would grade her on my top ten list of what I considered a great sexual experience. If the women did not have a clue or did not know what to do sexually to please me, I would grade her much lower on the list of my sexual memories.

Once affection and love entered in and became more of a reality in my life, this all soon changed. Sex is always a great attractant toward any occasion you might think of. However, it is always love that is the lasting emotion after sex is over that the heart appeals for when the touch of a real person of affection binds you to them.

In some cases, it is the desperate act of sex that makes life more frightening than anything that you can experience. Desperation will make an individual do what you never thought you would do or even search for the right affection in the wrong place or worst with the wrong person.

Desperation may cloud one's judgment and decisions of all future interactions that they may experience in life with that potential special someone. I was always told, "don't be desperate for a girl or a woman to come into your life; take your time and find a good one."

This saying means nothing when you consider yourself a young stud trying to find your way in life; you are young and crazy and have every answer under the stars of heaven. This perfectly described me (and so many other young men) that have their whole lives ahead of them but cannot appreciate the concept of patience until you lose it before you really understand its' worth.

I now know that true desperation is the ultimate deceiver when it comes to "contracting" Blue Ball Syndrome. It denies you the selection process of time and quality in a mate.

For example, have you ever got involved with a person and later, after a great waste of time, had to ask yourself, "how did I end up with that kind of guy or girl?"

If you have ever been there, you realize that you have been in a desperate phase when it came to this individual and once time and the experience have passed you realize that this is not what you want in your life anymore.

If this is or was you, please do not be alarmed. I cannot tell how many times that I have been in the desperate mode of my youthful days. I began to look for opportunities that were only meant to fulfill my sexual desires.

Sex in my mind depicted me as attractive, well-liked and powerful even if no one else saw or thought it. Desperation can take over at times when we are at our loneliest; that is not always a great feeling when you are searching for companionship.

I had to learn how to look for a female but not out of mere desperation. It is evident that every man and woman are emotional at times. These experiences allow us to be prepared for love, com-

Blue Ball Syndrome

mitment, passion and compromise in our relationships. People can trigger certain things in us by merely approaching us in a unique way that turn us on or a look that sends chills through our whole body.

Quite naturally, an intimate dinner or a surprise kiss may turn into a passionate embrace. Capturing a person's heart in a fleeting passing moment is one example of this. These are simple ways that our internal "emotional timers" are set and this causes us to become helpless creatures for affection from the people we crave emotionally or sexually because of lust or passion

In this case, a person may experience Blue Ball Syndrome when a person is at their peak of sexual arousal, eager for stimulation and yet the person you are pursuing is unable to fulfill your most intimate desires.

This is where many men and women can become extremely frustrated, especially if the man or woman has fixated on you as the ultimate desperate quest of passion and sexual satisfaction.

It has been documented that many crimes of passion come from the unsuspecting man or woman with no criminal record. However, this person was so full of desperation for another that once they were faced with heightened sexual arousals, in this state of passion, they have killed the man or woman they were pursuing in a desperate outburst moment of rage.

Unfortunately, stories of "death by passion" are truly real and happen all the time in our society. Hollywood thrives on the act of desperate lovers in a quarrel. It makes for a great movie headline and graphic novel; we crave to learn about how we love and how desperation controls the actions of others in society.

Desperation is played out in all the movies and in love novels such as Romeo and Juliet and many others. However, the human instinct of emotion is very real. My personal preference would be for someone to seek me out of love and not desperation. Love is usually not a model for such classic crimes that are seen with desperation.

Love has maturity and patience with it and has sometimes come with long suffering and in many cases even forgiveness.

I would always want to have love pursue me rather than a desperate girl with the ability to stalk me coming after me. I am sure that if it is sex you want, desperation will certainly deliver it to you. However, if love does not embrace you with proper satisfaction, then desperation can become a prison of your own affection for what we all want in life, the right combination of sexual satisfaction and great passion.

Adversely, this is the dark side of Blue Ball Syndrome where many can definitely see the difference between people that are desperate for sex versus people that desire you from their heart with love.

Knowing the person that I have now become in life, I would choose love any day. I am glad to be over the desperate side of life where sex was the ultimate thrill and love was just a lucky portion of the aftermath of my sexual quest.

Youth has its privileges in our lives where men and women can make good selections and allow their hearts to choose and not have scars to identify with it. Ironically, I am glad that life continues to evolve forward to season the mind and prepare the heart to recognize real love.

This allows mankind to know what life is about as we age. Maturity in life lets one learn to handle the effects of unfulfilled gratification (sexual and or otherwise) from the range of passion in desperation to the compromising, daily evolving cycle of love and development in our relationships with one another.

Chapter 8

LEARNING TO COMPROMISE FOR LOVE

Learning to compromise in marriage or relationships is the true secret to any real success of that marriage or relationship. The ability to compromise is a skill that is missing in many relationships that ultimately (all too often) dissolve in this country.

It has been proven that in many couples' lives, the ability to compromise has been seen as incredibly hard to do. Most importantly, if we are honest with ourselves, we like to have our way as we see it in more cases than not.

I will not lie to you and say that I have compromised with everything that my wife had put before me; quite naturally, that would be completely dishonest and would look totally out of character from a realistic point of view. In all honesty, I am still "in training" when it comes to learning to compromise with my wife regarding my own needs and desires.

I am amazed at how many people feel like they have made it to a level of accomplishment in life when they feel like the inability to argue or have disputes of any kind about where to eat or what color to paint the walls in the house is a good thing.

Blue Ball Syndrome

I am not familiar with any couple (or couples) where *everything* goes wonderful all the time. In fact, I cannot say that I have not had one argument with my wife; we have had several from little things like which pot to cook the food in, where to park the car and my all time favorite, which T.V. program to watch when we both have a program running at the same time.

Furthermore, I know I am not alone in this description of life with someone you love; it just comes with the territory. However, if my wife did not get on my nerves every now and then I would wonder, "What the hell is going on here?"

I say that because, in my life as I am sure in yours, a person gets used to opposing point of views with their spouse or special significant other. So, in times when they are not in opposition with you, it makes life seem boring and even lifeless because you actually miss that person's ability to be honest with you. This is the reason we love our spouses and girlfriends or boyfriends.

My friend Stan took a business trip for about a week to New York. He was literally lonely and felt horrible during that time he was away from his wife.

His wife was bossy and a real straight shooter in the home with him and he would usually say, "I need a vacation so I can get a break and just relax from home for awhile."

Ironically, the opportunity came for Stan to get away and take his vacation, just as he desired. Stan didn't have any children, so being away from his wife was the only person that he would be leaving home while on his vacation.

As Stan started his vacation, he survived two days without seeing his wife and he began to wonder how much he actually wanted to get away from her. However, when he had that time away from her, Stan started reflecting on how much he actually missed his wife.

Even though at home he talked about how much she would get on his nerves about little things, Stan loved his wife and her personality which is what he was drawn to. Stan realized without her that his world was boring and lonely and that his wife was really the life of his party and made his world feel good. After Stan's second day of dealing with his apparent loneliness, he contacted his wife and bought a plane ticket [for her] to New York for the weekend. It was a great compromise for him and a great time for his wife.

This was a great way for Stan to realize why he loved his wife, even though she disagreed with him on many things. He knew if he lost her, it meant the loss of what was happiness for him and satisfaction for his heart. This is the greatest lesson of all in love that will certainly keep sexual or emotional problems from overtaking a good relationship or marriage. This is what Stan had to learn as do many other men.

Remember, compromising is the resource that all relationships must utilize in order to survive. It

Blue Ball Syndrome

is a true test of wills when questioning your ability to compromise. As we see in Stan's case, if you cannot recognize the value of your spouse then you cannot recognize the apparent joy your spouse places in your life either.

It is the ability to submit your will at times for the happiness of the one you love that is the most challenging skill to learn. Compromising requires you to come out of your own selfish will for the satisfaction of someone that you deeply care for.

Consequently, this is not easy. But, it is essential for trust, sustainability of love and cooperation as a unit to survive the obstacles of daily living. Communication is the key ingredient to developing the skill of learning how to compromise.

If communication is not optimal in your relationship, then it will be easy to allow the sexual or emotional problems to direct you away from your spouse or significant other.

Many couples lose this skill early on during their relationship development years because they lack the essential skills to have sober and forthcoming communication with each other. With regards to marriage, this may explain why the national divorce rate in America today is a staggering 52%... *go figure*!

From an ethnic standpoint, it may possibly explain why over 72% of African-American children are born to single parent households. The loss of this skill may also explain why Caucasian/European households have increasingly grown into single parent households by 37% since 2008. In my home state of Tennessee, the national divorce rate is the second highest in the nation, following Arkansas.

It should be evident that compromising for love is essential to obtaining a happy life with a mate. This is a skill that takes daily practice in all relationships. While I am still *yet* in training, I can admit that I am much better today than I was yesterday and I will be better tomorrow than I am today. I simply hope all couples can strive for perfection when developing this skill even as I continue to do so in my own life.

Learn to value those you love and the skill of compromise. It makes the life journey of love easier as it evolves into something wonderful once selfishness has been removed from your relationship.

Chapter 9

SHOW ME WHAT YOU WANT ME TO DO

This is a real appeal to all relationships and marriages! It is a call for honesty and openness in what attracts you to your boyfriend, girlfriend, wife or husband. This chapter opens one's mind to the possibility of entertaining what you want from your significant other and more importantly, what you want them to do for you. As the reader, I must ask the question "have you *ever* told your lover what you really like for them to do when it comes to satisfying you, sexually or otherwise?" Try not to look away shyly or close the book now. Be honest and admit it that I have your attention (uh...huh, you know who you are).

In an effort to be honest with your mate, my best advice is to just say what is on your mind. Most of our lovers and significant others desire to know what satisfies us. A person can only give you what you want and need when you express what's on your mind.

In many instances, we spend so much time trying to figure out what a person may want without asking them what they want. Men (especially) do not want to be caught dead asking a woman what she wants us to do sexually especially after talking up a "good game" to just get them on a date. My friend Jamal stopped me in the hallway the other day. Jamal is an interesting guy that lives down the street and has a beautiful girlfriend named Sabrina (she is drop dead gorgeous).

From a physical standpoint, most men would eagerly embrace the opportunity to be with Sabrina sexually.

I asked Jamal one day, "man...have you ever asked her what she likes for you to do with her sexually?" Jamal sat back and said, "hell no, are you crazy man?!? That will give away your areas of inexperience with the opposite sex."

Jamal continued, "Women, expect us guys to know that shit man; I mean they are coming to you because you have presented them with the illusion that you know what you are doing. If you ask a girl something like that, then you look weak and like a beginner to a woman."

I really pondered what Jamal had said and I, like many other guys, did not want to look weak or inexperienced to the ladies in my experiences so I played the game if I got with a girl.

I would kiss and fool around with her going with the flow, never knowing what she liked sexually or did not want me to do to make her time with me much better and more memorable. This is the type of girl that I would get a call from every now and then.

Finally, after seeing that I was not always successful in my quest as a young man for a good, stable relationship, I ran into Dr. Nelson, a Psy-

Blue Ball Syndrome

chologist that taught a class in human social evolution and sexuality. Her analysis of why sex is great and how it works in relationships was totally different from Jamal's and it made so much sense to me as I sought more understanding on the subject.

According to Dr. Nelson, men have built up the mentality that they are the champions of sex and the allure of sexual bliss reigns in the penis. To Dr. Nelson, this was totally a misconception of thought. It seems that many men get there lessons of sex and intimacy from other men who generally lie about there sexual conquest of females from their pasts.

This also comes from visual contributions such as movies and even musical messages of domination over females. In Jamal's case he was a dominant male that played up the image that he knew how to do all sorts of sexual acts with his girlfriend and because he has a beautiful woman on his arm, everyone perceives that he is great in bed when it comes to pleasing her.

Dr. Nelson pointed out one thing that I never even considered. She stated, "I bet Jamal has never told you about how he makes his relationship work to keep his beautiful girlfriend. He may tell you one thing but even the "great Jamal" is finding other ways to keep his woman in the bed with him as all men and women have to do to keep that passion burning."

Dr. Nelson pointed out that men like Jamal have found a way to say one thing in public and do the exact opposite behind closed doors. Based on this theory, a good relationship must exist with knowing what your lover likes in their pursuit of satisfaction.

Questions must be asked in such a way that stimulates your love but does not offend or pull them away from the passionate direction you're attempting to go. This is one of the exciting parts of any relationship.

According to Dr. Nelson, a man or woman can really be creative in how they approach their lover. For example, over the course of dinner or a nice walk in the park is always a great way to open the door of your lover's mind to find out how and what they think about you when it comes to sexual experiences and romance. What man or woman doesn't want to be asked what satisfies them sexually? **_Their answers may actually surprise you!_**

Dr. Nelson states, "when you are into a person where romance and sexual interest is in the air, the allure of what pleases your partner is the ultimate turn on and will increase the sexual intimacy. Once each person's needs are met, any experience with this person is a real high point and the arousal factor is at its peak because you now know what your partner wants from you. It is amazing when two people can unlock the potential in their hidden desires. When unknown sexual intimacy is no more a mystery, then you have a map before you and it is

Blue Ball Syndrome

only time, energy and the availability of space that is your barrier at this point."

Dr. Nelson's talk made it all very simple for me to understand and put some of her techniques into practice in my own life. I shared Dr. Nelson's wisdom with my wife and even my friend Jamal.

He said, "you know, Dr. Nelson was right, I began asking Sabrina what she wanted sexually and she totally responded."

Jamal continued, "we had a nice dinner that I cooked for her the other night and I asked her, "Sabrina what is it that you like for me to do with you sexually that you enjoy the most?"

Sabrina replied, "Jamal, I like it when you kiss me on my neck and down my stomach and kiss my thighs and suck my nipples the way you do." Sabrina continued, "I love how you perform oral sex on me and how you hold my legs on your shoulders as you penetrate into me slowly yet gently; that is amazing to me. I feel my body totally into you when you do that to me and I am so aroused that I have at least three orgasms like that and it feels so good to me Jamal."

Jamal said, "Doc, from there I swear we barely finished my dinner meal, I was so aroused as we ate our food that I crawled under the table to her and gently kissed her thighs as she said she liked for me to do."

Jamal continued, "I slid off her panties and sat her back in the chair at the dinner table and tasted her warmth. It was great and Sabrina wrapped her legs around me as I could hear her calls of passion and satisfaction as I kissed and licked Sabrina with great enthusiasm. I knew this was what she wanted me to do and loved for me to do to please her. I just wanted to feel her release and express her gratitude for me just wanting to please her."

Jamal continued, "I picked up Sabrina in my arms and took her to my bedroom and I completely undressed her as she kissed me on my neck and down my stomach as well. Sabrina grabbed me and performed oral sex on me and I went crazy, wow! I told Sabrina earlier at dinner that I enjoyed her kissing me on my neck and I wanted her to perform oral sex on me and make me enjoy the pleasure of it. Man, did she ever come through with that request as well. Sabrina was not one to be rushed. She massaged me totally with her whole beautiful body and I felt like a king, Doc."

Jamal continued, "The candles were burning and had reached their peak of burning as we continued our love making. That really turned me on because I could look at Sabrina and feel her whole body. Sabrina loves me to grab her legs and enter in, my body on her body, and kiss her while embracing each other at the same time, it is just heaven man."

I was glad that I told Jamal what Dr. Nelson said. It seemed Dr. Nelson's wisdom worked for Jamal very well.

I was happy that I learned a good secret myself about how to ask my wife about things that I

Blue Ball Syndrome

wanted to try at home to improve our romantic and sexual experiences. It seems that all couples can learn from this and be more open and honest about what they want from their partner.

In my opinion, it enhances the passion and keeps certain problems associated with Blue Ball Syndrome from having its place in your home. I would rather be in a stable relationship knowing my lover or spouse could satisfy me rather than be in a relationship where my sexual satisfaction was based on guess work and my ultimate desires were never shared with my lover or spouse; that would be a horrible experience.

However, many couples deal with this out of fear of rejection and the embarrassment of learning what they took for granted in assuming they know their significant other sexually. Dr. Nelson was right, you have to be honest with what you want from your lover or spouse sexually because if you want a monogamous relationship, then you want to know how to keep your lover or spouse aroused, satisfied and looking forward to the next time. Taking the advice of Dr. Nelson, I plan on telling my wife what I like over a nice dinner.

I am preparing a home cooked meal of baked chicken, spinach with some aerating potatoes and some dinner rolls. I'm even going to bake and prepare chocolate cake for dessert. My wife will be surprised when she sees the candles glowing at the table and the kids are safely at my in-laws for the night. The atmosphere is set with jazz music playing in the background, the table is all set in addition to serving her chilled dinner wine. I know that my wife likes home cooked meals because she told me (particularly one that includes baked chicken).

According to Dr. Nelson, this evening should go exceptionally well because I have set the environment to have open communication with my wife. Tonight will be a night where we both can be open and honest about likes and dislikes. After dinner and dessert, we'll see where the night takes us.....

Chapter 10

MARRIED, BUT THE PLAYER STILL REMAINS...WHAT NOW?!?

This chapter exposes those who are married, not in a relationship and find that marriage can be a real trip down the valley of the unknown. This chapter is a challenging one because it forces a married couple or individuals in marriages to be honest with themselves about how the marriage is surviving.

No one really wants to air out marital problems to the world and neither should any couple feel they have to. However, if you are married and have felt the separation of love and passion in your marriage, then this chapter is really for you. Experiencing a lack of emotional and/or physical connection happens all too often in marriages. Many wrestle with the concept of I am married yet I still have attractions for another man or woman.

Well, that is perfectly normal. Being married does not make you blind to people that you see every day or to even attractive people that you observe around the work place.

In fact, I would say that when you are married, people around you and at work that you were attracted to before you got married are still attractive to you. The difference is, you have chosen someone in the crowd of people that you knew to be the significant other in your life. That says a lot about what you are attracted to and what led to your decision to choose the individual you chose to become your spouse.

To gain a better understanding of this, we first must look at what an individual is attracted to and that will really help us find out why a married individual still is attracted to others but is yet married.

Most people marry for three top reasons according to a recent internet responder survey (2008). The area that received the highest response was physical attraction as to what led people choose what they wanted in a spouse. Other survey results included love for the person, happiness with that person and overall attraction of what you wanted in a mate.

These are the primary reasons most people listed in a survey of why married individuals got married. This survey was conducted using a control group of 3,218 people. This survey tells us many things as to how and why people choose marital partners.

Many couples married because they were physically attracted to each other at first and this led to love and in-depth feelings for their partner. However, the survey results reveal the critical answer that attraction and not love or deep affection is

Blue Ball Syndrome

what drives many people toward love for another and not the other way around.

The survey demonstrates how individuals that choose spouses based on physical attraction first will be the more outgoing, flirtatious and people-friendly individuals that many people find attractive, warm and even marriage material based on their personality and ability to appeal to other people. This characteristic trait is a great one to possess but it also may cause one to ask the question could this individual with these traits that chose you for your looks and personality believe that your looks and personality will ultimately satisfy this individual in a consistent way once in a committed marriage.

Once this question is asked, married individuals must seek to answer the question, "can individuals who are married resist temptation of being attracted to someone even though they are in a committed marriage to someone else?" Just the mere mention of this question begins to create a sense of tension and melodrama in discussion groups, book clubs, television talk shows and national radio programs.

From the images we see plastered each evening on the television, what is perceived as beauty is a big problem in America because for most people, particularly women, the idea of what is considered to be beautiful is based on how much more physically attractive one woman is in comparison to another woman.

Because of this, it is a real challenge for most women to keep their husband's eyes and attention solely on her.

Naturally, this can go both ways. When women see men on the job who are masculine and toned shapely bodies, very well dressed and well groomed, that instant attraction may easily develop into lust without any warning. It seems that visual temptation is the culprit that influences most husbands and wives to compete with societies definition of what is considered attractive. A simple trip to the local supermarket barrages a person's mind with articles and images that offers tips on how to keep your waistline smaller through dieting or how to diminish wrinkles to look youthful again.

Women are becoming increasingly wise to the fact that men are visual and are attracted to what they see, married or not. Because of this, the underlying question remains as to "just how attractive should a woman remain in her mate's eyes in order to prevent him from being tempted once they are married?"

Women are not the only ones bombarded with advertisements to become a better you; men are often subjected to this as well. Naturally, if a woman can be tempted with an attractive man, surely her husband can be tempted as well with a gorgeous female. For men, tabloids offer suggestions such as not letting your hair become gray is a great way to maintain your attractiveness to women.

Blue Ball Syndrome

Subliminal and overt advertising techniques suggest that neither men nor women desire a mate or companion that has allowed themselves to go and become old looking and unattractive.

If society would have its' way, most married people would consistently be told that you are getting too old and that your marriage is a constant battle competing with someone (male or female) that is younger and in better physical shape than you are. Many people believe that married people have it easy because they can have someone at home and yet have an outside life as well. Many say this does not involve sex, but merely flirtation.

Flirtation is the name of the game in social play and interaction nowadays. Some people feel that being nice is a form of flirtation. For example, a married man may see a female get on an elevator with him and he notices her wearing a unique dress that she obviously doesn't wear all the time and simply says to her "hey how are you doing today? By the way, you look nice in your dress."

Now, some see this as a harmless greeting and being nice and merely offering a compliment towards a co-worker. It cannot be assumed that this married man was trying to hit on this woman or trying to try strike up a conversation. Nor should it be assumed that the husband is cheating on his wife. He is simply complimenting a co-worker on her dress and no other exchange took place with this compliment. Would this be defined as a flirtatious exchange?

Yes, it would be. Is it harmless? Again the answer is yes! Does it mean that this husband is a player? No, not at all!

On the other hand, if a married man gets on the elevator with a female colleague and proceeds with same conversation yet takes it another step further by saying "maybe one day we can have lunch sometimes and catch up with each other, let me know when you can be available", then his actions would be considered open flirtation with a possible undertone of hinting around a possible romantic or sexual interlude.

It is obvious that this husband is attracted to this female and he is obviously into her attire, figure and beauty and he is already laying out the welcome mat for a lunch date and possibly an eventual sexual encounter as well. This is the husband in "player mode" that many wives dread and even fear showing up in their marriages. This is also the setting of a scenario that naturally occurs.

It is obvious that many affairs happen with people that we see and are attracted to and covet all the time. The perception that the "the grass is greener on the other side" gives the illusion that what we see is much better than what we have in our marriage. Not only is this untrue, but it also detrimental to your relationship.

This scenario also works both ways. A wife that has a good husband that is attractive, very sociable, polite and courteous may be tempted as well. One day she is at the office and a gentleman approaches

Blue Ball Syndrome

her and says, "How are you doing today? I saw you and just thought I would introduce myself. I admire your work and I hope I can learn some good pointers from your expertise. I look forward to working with you."

As you can see, this is merely harmless and a normal business introduction within normal conversational limits in the work place. Does the man admire the wife in this scenario? Of course he does, but does he press the issue of trying to attract this female into some sexual affair, no. He does not present that in this scenario.

However, to be fair as in the husband's case, we must show how this wife can be approached sexually and flirtatiously as well. Let me be clear as well as just. It is not a woman's fault when she is deemed attractive to other men. This also applies to men who are able to attract other women as well.

In this scenario, we are looking at a gentleman approaching this attractive wife in her office at the work place. We shall see how the table turns and how the wife is approached by a sexually flirtatious gentleman in the work place.

A wife is in her office and a nice well-dressed gentlemen notices her doing her work and he admires her work and notices how naturally attractive this wife is. He approaches her and says, "How are you doing today? I saw you in your office and I hope I am not disturbing you. I am a great admirer of your work and I can see why you are so successful.

I hope I can learn some of your skills on my up and coming projects." The gentleman continues, "I was hoping that we could talk more and maybe you can join me for lunch sometime, I would like to get to know you a little better. I find you very attractive and I like your personality." The wife replied, "I am married, so I am not going to be able to give you what you want in that kind of way. But I do thank you for the compliment on my work."

As you can see, this gentleman is obviously very attracted to this woman who is married, successful and quite naturally appeals to this gentlemen's sexual nature. Many people may choose to describe him as a player. By all accounts (and also based on his actions), that would be a befitting title for this gentlemen.

However, what this scenario tells us is that to be attractive is not illegal nor can we take blame for men who see our wives as attractive and vice versa for husbands that are able to attract other women to their masculine and professional success that most women admire in men. It is not a wife's fault that men find her professional and successful and attractive to look upon.

That type of wife is a compliment to the man that she is married to. Some people would say that this attractive woman that is married would be classified as a player; however, this is not true. How we can blame the woman for attracting other men to her just for being a woman that is intelligent, successful and also attractive?

Blue Ball Syndrome

In my opinion, people who are not married have the flirtatious radar in a continuous "on" mode that allows them to be sociable because many are trying to attract a spouse and flirting is a part of the courtship process.

Moreover, flirting does not mean that married people are players either. It means that they are married but recognize that communicating with others outside of their marriage is important to maintain any personable relationship.

Harmless flirting is how many people congratulate and even celebrate events around those persons we work with and socially mingle with in our daily lives. It does not mean that every married man or woman is trying to have an affair.

It should be made clear that everyone has a natural ability to attract someone no matter how unattractive you may think that you are. Someone will always find you attractive and will try to act on that attraction for you. That is not your fault, it is the natural selection of genetics with skin color, hair type, body make up (shape), eye color and character traits that captivate the human psyche and draw others to you.

When married people open the door to the proposal of those who are attracted to them, this may lead to so many problems. Blue Ball Syndrome may occur in these flirtatious situations when the married person is enticed and engaged in a form of seduction that makes the non-married pursuer more attractive than the spouse.

This can be where the "player" in the married individual is usually exposed. They entertain the idea of an affair, only avoiding the opportunity of this chance encounter in efforts to overcome a negative outcome of the potential affair.

Consequently, once this situation presents itself in a marriage it can lead to roads that are never meant to be chartered in married life. Players in marriages can be individuals' that have gone rogue which subsequently defy the rules associated with being a married individual. However, there is hope for the player even in a marriage.

Most people are enticed by what they were originally attracted to in the first place before they got married. In order to turn this around, the player must become refocused to find a reason (or something) that causes him or her to demonstrate a level of attraction for their spouse they elected to choose over all other potential candidates.

Curiosity is normal for any person that is married or not, but the player is an opportunist that allows curiosity to become a way to have an affair or simply a sexual conquest outside of the marriage itself.

People flirting in marriages is a common thing and they are not always seeking to find an affair or have a sexual encounter with someone outside of their marriage.

Most people are very faithful in their marriages and just like to flirt and complement those that live their lives in a totally different manner. The flirtation may be harmless, but this does not have to become a divisive issue between spouses. It is my opinion that if you have married a person that is a social butterfly/player, don't try to change them or make them change their style of who they are.

It seems that this characteristic is what attracted you to your spouse in the first place. Customarily, this person will be a very outgoing professional male or female that enjoys a large group of colleagues and friends that like to be around them because of their energy and attractive personality.

This does not have to mean that they are overly flirtatious or are having an outside affair. To enjoy this type of individual, you must become a part of their world and enjoy what they enjoy.

Remember, this individual married you for a reason and you are the attractant that has caught their eye and ultimately their heart as well. The power of the marriage and the attractant of the player in your spouse lie within whatever power you possess from the time that your spouse chose to marry you.

Once you find what it is that made your spouse crazy about you and get back to that special appeal of your heart, you will become that significant, attracting element that your spouse will respond to with full attention. If it is music, play their song. If it's love making, make love like it is your last day alive, as you did back in the days without any drama.

If it is quiet time needed, put the kids to bed and spend time together like you did before the kids were born. If its' affection that is needed, hold your spouse's hand like you did when you were younger and kiss your spouse in public and tell them they are special to you all the time, even in the presence of friends and colleagues.

Take your spouse out to lunch sometimes; occasionally, get dressed and take your spouse out to a nice ball or gala with a live band or good music and get your groove on. I think that all spouses like that. Take a vacation like a cruise and live it up on a nice Caribbean island somewhere. I don't know any spouse that cannot appreciate that!

Go to church and eat dinner together as often as you can. Take a walk in the park and go to the movies together. Make a date out of going to the kids events like ball games and theatre productions the kids have while in school.

Plan trips around the family when you can so the kids will see you hug and kiss each other and learn how to solve conflicts by watching their parents solve their issues lovingly and peacefully with each other.

Get your spouse or significant other a card just because, for no special reason. Cards always make any special person feel good. Lastly, cook at home as often as you can. This will save money for the family and builds an intimate time for the family and also for the spouses.

Blue Ball Syndrome

Remember the advice of Dr. Nelson as well and I believe you and your "player" spouse will be just fine; *have fun rekindling your relationship*!

Chapter 11

WHY COUPLES NEED COUNSELING EVEN WHEN NOTHING IS WRONG

Blue Ball Syndrome has been explained throughout the previous chapters and it is evident that if a marriage or relationship is not truly grounded in love that the day-to-day life struggles of that union's existence will surely kill the spirit of any marriage or relationship.

Emphatically, many professional Theologians, Clinical Psychologists and Family Marital Therapists all agree that having a group of counselors around is a good idea for any relationship or marriage. This is like having a safety protocol to act as a survival mechanism for any challenge that may confront the marriage.

Having someone to talk to that you and your significant other are familiar with is a great additional element to any marriage or relationship. It only adds to the solidarity of the marriage or relationship and it helps to secure the harmony of the two people involved. This keeps a three-chord community around the concept of love and devotion that acts like a band of emotional integrity that upholds the family in good and challenging times of the relationship or marriage.

Blue Ball Syndrome

Many couples use religion or their faith as an additional tool to keep the relationship or marriage in a progressive mode even in a non-challenging time of the marriage or relationship. This gives the couple a place to worship and pray and strengthen each other together by allowing stress and frustration to be left at an outside place like an altar, synagogue or mosque. These are the institutions that promote forgiveness, survival for marriage, positive relationships and harmony in the family. These religious edifices also promote many family oriented functions that couples can enjoy together. This exalts the primary function of togetherness in a therapeutic community fashion. Ironically, this helps the marriage or relationship and other couples share in the challenges and the joys of the marriage or relationship.

Couples in marriages and relationships should use what they have learned from loving one another to strengthen their mate by reassuring one another of their ability to survive from past experiences. Consistently, this will remind the couple of their history and the legacy of survival that usually builds unity throughout the course of time with the marriage or relationship. This is an element in a relationship that can be experienced throughout the good and challenging times of a marriage or relationship that enables an inner strength to emerge, this is a continuing force of recognition in love between two people.

It seems that relationships are about the times we share with our significant others and have family around, these ultimately enrich our lives and serve as the catalyst to any great love story. Advisedly, one can only benefit from having a family structure in place in which everyone contributes to the betterment of the family unit in ways such as alleviating stress and also by honoring family traditions for generations to come.

Maintaining a strong familial structure is the foundation of all great marriages and relationships. Cultural and customary identity is the central focus of most marriages and relationships. Unique customs such as not only learning but also teaching how to prepare a favorite family dish or meal is just an example of a custom that if shared and passed down will solidify the foundation of the overall family structure through bonding, sharing and invoking a sense of familial unity.

In situations where the foundation of the familial unit appear to be on shaky ground, having access to a great support system such as friendships is always a good resource of initial counseling and comfort to any married couple or individuals in a relationship.

Friends are the fabric that reflects who we are in our lives. Ironically, friends are our time gaps and foundational pieces of life opportunity that help relationships and marriages maintain ties to some-

Blue Ball Syndrome

thing greater within each of us and our relationships.

On a personal note, my friends were a part of my life when I needed them as I went through a challenge in my own marriage. I was amazed at how my friends became living life rafts as my marriage was confronted with Blue Ball Syndrome. I seriously thought about ending my marriage and dealing with the after affects of being alone.

Believe me, I was just that upset and disgusted. If it were not for friends that counseled both my wife and myself, believe me, I would not have been able to write this book. My life testimonies would be something totally different than what they are today.

Friends were my primary counselors that helped me to relate and even cope with an intrusive force that challenged the core of my marriage and tested my deepest resolve that I never imagined I would ever have to face. If my friends were not planted at the inner core of my life, I cannot imagine how I would have survived this ordeal and remained married.

It took friends that not only knew me and my wife, but those that were willing to understand our state of mind and our situation to counsel us through our challenging times. This became a great source of strength and vitality for me as I began to regroup in my life and heal from my marital challenges.

In retrospect, my friends offered a great sense of stress relief and spiritual guidance once the decision was made to restore my marriage.

Couples that are able to laugh and forgive will have a better fighting chance of surviving any challenges to the marriage or relationship. Forgiveness is a healing balm that must be applied daily in relationships.

Many couples are amazed once they realize that each must practice forgiveness daily in order to achieve the benefits of conflict resolution in their relationship when compared to those that choose not to effectively communicate. Blue Ball Syndrome affects a marriage or relationship the most when communication has been abandoned and loneliness sets in, and physically, as well as psychologically separates the husband and wife.

Understandably, this opens the door for an easy plan of escape from the marriage and into the arms of an outside individual to fill the apparent void in the relationship.

It is imperative that couples make a worthwhile effort to maintain open lines of communication and emotional ties and maintain daily forgiveness if an offense has occurred within their relationships. It has been demonstrated by most psychologists and psychiatrists that communication and effective efforts of patience, kindness, understanding and daily devotion to meeting each other's needs (both emotionally and physically) is a comprehensive key toward survival in relationships and marriage.

Blue Ball Syndrome

In fact, even the bible itself explains about how married couples are not to be away from each other too long even after dedication to prayer because it can open the opportunity for loneliness and temptation to invade in a relationship and take its toll (I Corinthians 7:5-6).

Effective communication demonstrated through caring and listening seems to be a unique formula that has been the strength of many couples that have been married for over 10 years. It is estimated that if a couple can make it past the first 5 years, there is a fighting chance they will learn how to survive for many more years to come.

On the contrary, if a couple has not learned how to survive this initial time period then various forms of Blue Ball Syndrome will certainly take its toll in the relationship. Indicators of relationship problems can be a combination of depravity due to loneliness, neglect, abandonment and betrayal of a relationship or marriage.

In my research for this book, many couples believed the term "Blue Ball Syndrome" was an old cliché; however, its' effects are extremely real and can make any couple act out in diverse forms of desperation for affection, love and a sense of belonging to someone that values who they are and what they have to offer.

This can occur even if that someone is a complete stranger that temporarily removes the signs of Blue Ball Syndrome and provide a sense of emotional or physical release or comfort.

Ironically, this is why men and women seek pleasure outside of their home that is not found in the home anymore. The division of couples through loneliness and neglect without intimacy, of any kind, is like cancer to the psyche of anyone that relies on their spouse or significant other for emotional support and physical companionship through emotional reassurance or sexual intimacy and of a couple's dedication towards their relationship or marriage.

In comparison, couples that practice sexual intimacy frequently and have positive, effective communication techniques, through quiet time where the children are put to bed and the couple can talk and cuddle is essential for proper psychological growth to limit stress and anxiety in a marriage or relationship.

These much needed (and desired) forms of communication allow each person in the relationship or marriage to become a complete and functioning unit that connects in a very dependent way where each relies on their partner for physical and emotional support. This helps to keep the man and woman from feeling neglected or even lonely when their spouse is around you. I personally like the Bible's interpretation of this subject as it reads,

The wife does not have authority over her own body
but the
husband does; likewise, the husband does not have authority

Blue Ball Syndrome

over his own body, but the wife does. Do not deprive one another
except perhaps by agreement for a set time, to devote yourselves
to prayer, and then come together again, so that Satan may not
tempt you because of your lack of self control." (Corinthians 7:3-5).

Therefore, having consistent communication both physically and with open, honest conversation is even advised by the Bible itself. As an adjunctive tool, meaningful counselors serve in support capacities to your marriage or relationship to teach good measures of how you are to cope in your relationship.

Taking a closer look at what "true" Blue Ball Syndrome really means and its effects on couples and even my own life has made me see myself better as a man, a husband and now even a father.

I pray that this work will shed light on your relationship or marriage and help you also navigate successfully through life's challenges of marriage and relationships. It is important that all couples maintain open lines of communication and physical appeal for each other.

Most importantly, couples must keep in mind that daily communication is key and paramount to the survival of any relationship even without a challenge to the relationship.

A great physical relationship incorporating sexual intimacy practices is a critical component for all couples to maintain continued success in their relationships. It is the basic human touch that is the assurance of life and intimacy in a relationship. Above all, forgiveness as a daily practice too must be incorporated in order to maintain a healthy relationship void of any symptoms associated with Blue Ball Syndrome. On a personal note, as the author of this book, I am currently divorced. However, I am happy, content and optimistic about finding love, joy and peace of mind with someone special in my future. It is true that good friends and wise counsel are beneficial to marriages and relationships even when nothing is wrong.

Chapter 12

WHY MEN AND WOMEN NEED A WEEKEND HIATUS/RECOVERY TRIP

It is often said, "I need a break away from my husband, wife, kids and the life I have just to get back to myself."

Many people at one time or another have uttered those exact words. My in-depth research preparing to write this book has caused me to notice that this sentiment is not only true but is also often needed in relationships to keep the vitality of the relationship whole. I elected to interview 30 men and 30 women for this chapter.

All interviewees are over the age of 27 and all are in stable relationships. 12 of the women were married and 18 were single but in a relationship longer than a year. 7 of the men that participated were married and 5 were divorced. 18 were in relationships greater than a year. 8 of the male interviewees had children while 12 of the female participants had children.

The diversity of the participants represented the American culture at its best as it stands today. 30% of the male participants were White males, 40% were African American and 30% were Latino and/or of Biracial decent. 25% of the female participants were Caucasian, 38% were African-American, 17% were Korean-American and 10% of Latino-American decent.

As one can see, the survey participants represent a great mixture of the values and customs associated with each heritage. The median age of 27 was chosen based on my experience that most men and women have agreed they feel more in control of their lives at this point and independent of the immature decision making processes associated with the early twenties and post-collegiate years.

The study results were very unique as it demonstrated what different ethnic, educational and socioeconomic backgrounds could relate to. The responses to the question in the study in no way reflect a cultural norm or generality of any nationality or racial group that participated.

My express intent was only to focus on the individual human social factors of how our American society views relationships and the importance of the strategy one chooses to use in order to maintain a healthy relationship based on social interactions of individuals of varying backgrounds as it relates to maintaining the original expectations of one's relationship.

Study participants were asked the question, "Do you believe that men and women should have a hiatus or recovery period from a relationship in order to help maintain a relationship?" Many of the participants felt that a loving relationship was a real chore and to maintain that relationship takes a

Blue Ball Syndrome

lot of work, social compromise and a willingness of allowing one person to often release their frustration and opinions by demonstrating patience to hear what your partner had to say.

The survey also opened the door to the question as to which person was actually serving in the dominant capacity in the relationship and ultimately, whose decision it would be that either partner can go on a hiatus or get away.

Ultimately, over 87% of the participants agreed that a hiatus or recovery period in a relationship should be granted to a spouse or significant other in order to salvage a good relationship.

Over 86% of the female participants stated that if the marriage or relationship demonstrated potential and just ran into volatile times that created stress, it was often encouraged that the woman should be given sometime, without pressure, to come to some conclusion to determine if the relationship was healthy enough to continue forward or leave due to irreconcilable differences.

95% of the male participants suggested that either the male or the female partner should be allowed to go for a while on hiatus from a relationship. Most men stated that a time limit should be placed on the hiatus, with time limits beginning at a weekend but not exceeding a week to resolve the issues.

It seems that many men often agreed that this time apart is a way to vent frustration and calm undesired feelings that often can escalate to more violent and highly stressed emotions between partners even in loving relationships. Moreover, the females also agreed on a time limit away emphasizing that if it takes more than a weekend or a week to decide on a relationship with someone or the value of it, then that partner of the relationship is usually a toxic non-compromising individual that will never change his or her ways.

This unfortunate revelation will always usher in a selfish vindicated attitude of why the relationship should always feel one-sided, naturally on the side of the person typically at fault. It seems that many marriages unfortunately end in divorce in America. It is estimated that over 50% of American marriages fail within 5 years of the vows being exchanged. In our study, 5 of the divorced men decided to talk about why they got divorced and how issues plagued their relationships. It was interesting and refreshing to hear from previously married men and what they had in common.

To be fair and balanced the 5 married women were also allowed to express dialog on the subject of a weekend hiatus. I first asked the men, "Can you tell me why your marriage failed?"

One of the participants responded, "My marriage failed because my ex-wife was stubborn and stuck in her own ways of doing things and it led to our unfortunate failure even to the point of ruining my family life with my kids."

A second male responded, "Well you know, when two people cannot get along or see eye to eye it causes problems even when you still love the person very much. I find my marriage failed because my wife and I just grew apart and probably never ever knew each other to the point where we felt like strangers to each other, quite naturally my sexual attraction at that point was not with my wife any more but was with the other woman that I am with now. So, I filed for divorce based on irreconcilable differences, we were just tired of trying after such a chaotic relationship of 6 years."

A third male responded, "My marriage failed because I found out that my wife was cheating on me with another man." The room fell silent with his statement; I could feel the tension grow as the third divorced male participant continued. "I was married for 12 years and my ex-wife had a daughter from a previous relationship. We were good friends and chatted often about many things and she was a couple years younger than me. I was 25 at this time of my life. Well, shortly after we were married, I began to see our life decrease in enjoyment. We had our first child after our 2nd year of marriage and I was happy and I believed my ex-wife was happy too. However, money got tight when I graduated from college and could not get a job in my field for quite some time and the stress of our relationship got the best of us."

The third man continued with a sigh of memorable frustration in his voice, "I could tell this was not the life that I planned for my ex-wife at that time or my baby as well. I noticed that my ex-wife began revisiting her hometown on weekends or often she would drive away and tell me she would be right back and would not come home until the next day. I would be worried sick especially if she kept my daughter out with her as well. As a father, I am sure most men feel the same. My ex-wife would say she was at her girlfriend's place or at her cousin's house that lived across town. One night, I followed her just by coincidence and lo and behold she went to her ex-boyfriend's place. I felt betrayed because she was there all night. I called her on her phone and she picked it up and I asked her where are you and are you coming home tonight?" She replied, "I am at my mothers and I will be home in the morning; it's late and I am going to stay here tonight."

I cannot tell you how devastated I was that she would lie to me and I had proof, I took a picture of her leaving her ex-boyfriend's house and kissing him deeply as they walked together down the block. I filed for divorced that week and won my case against her. I now have joint custody of my daughter." He continued, "If the hiatus recovery situation was an option I would have been the first to use it. But when someone is not making you feel they are worth that allotted time and effort in a relationship then working it out with time away would have still resulted in my ex-wife cheating on me as she did.

Besides, I too was having sex with females and getting my satisfaction I could not get at home with

Blue Ball Syndrome

a few women here and there. So, I do not feel it would have helped us in our marriage. I actually had a few sexual encounters with my ex-wife's girlfriend and she knew I was married but her friend performed oral sex on me in my car one night after me and my ex-wife had an argument. I know it was wrong but, I must admit, it felt good releasing my frustration into my ex-wife's friend like that. I felt I was getting back at my ex-wife through her girlfriend that was more understanding to me and showing me some sympathy, I guess.

We continued a sexual relationship usually when my ex-wife and I would argue. I started meeting her at hotels and bars and it was a release that I enjoyed especially knowing my wife was cheating on me as well. But, I never mentioned it to my ex-wife. This all happened after everything started going downhill and eventually I caught her cheating on me. But, our relationship was over long ago. Catching her cheating did not even make me mad that day in-fact; I used it as fuel to find a divorce lawyer. I still maintained a sexual relationship with her friend every now and then. This girlfriend is still hanging out with my ex-wife up to today. Now, it is just mindless screwing around, but no love is there; just great sex when I want it."

I was really shocked to hear that story from the third divorced man in the group. It seemed as if he still had some issues with the divorce and yet wanted a form of revenge toward his ex-wife. The rest of the divorced men decided not to share their stories of why they got divorced but agreed that the weekend hiatus that cooled down stress and tension and allowed each side to have some private and personal time would have probably helped before a separation or divorce would have happened in their lives. It was now time for the women to speak....

Surprisingly, all of the women agreed as well that the weekend hiatus or recovery period was a healthy thing for a marriage even if things are going well in the relationship. It appears that the female participants in the group that were all single, never married and had no children at all observed that relationships that did not smother one another or had a great sense of trust built into them lasted longer. Besides, these are model marriages that people were actually proud of and wanted to be in. One of the women, named Greta, spoke of a time when in a previous relationship her boyfriend did not trust her to spend time away with her family and got angry with her when she wanted to stay out one night after her girlfriends birthday party.

Greta stated, "I would rather have an allotted space built in to my future relationships for some freedom and trust not to be tied down like in a marriage to someone that I am not married too. That is crazy and I'll be by myself before I try to hold on to a man that wants to dominate and control me."

I replied, "I can truly understand where you are coming from, it seems like the weekend hiatus or

Blue Ball Syndrome

recovery act which is voluntary would at least be a buffer to allow someone the room to know what they wanted in a relationship as well."

Another female participant named Kendra agreed with my statement and added to the conversation. "I feel that if the divorced men here would have used that option, not saying that the weekend hiatus or recovery period is the answer to divorce or a failing relationship, but, it is an alternative if two people can somehow see a sense of worth to try to maintain a relationship."

Kendra continued, "It also takes two people who can be mature about matters and come to some form of agreement to coexist through challenging times. It appears that in many relationships these days when someone is ready to get out of a relationship, the individual who is fed up has already begun to start other relationships to get away from the "terrible" one [relationship] they want out of."

I replied, "That is often true Kendra. Have you ever had any difficult times where the hiatus or recovery period could be helpful for you in your current relationship?"

Kendra laughed and sighed and then replied, "Oh yea, my boyfriend is nice and kind to me but we have had our moments, believe me; it has not been all peaches and cream all the time. Before I heard of your hiatus/recovery act, I actually took one weekend and it did make all the difference in the world. I did not know that it was a proposed item that was suggested by professional counselors as an option to the drama that comes from dealing with another human being that you love."

The room fell silent to hear that Kendra had actually used this hiatus/recovery act in her relationship before and to know that it helped was a real revelation, knowing that if someone did use the technique it would salvage a relationship. What a coincidence that someone who was a part of this discussion would have discovered that!

I then asked, "Well Kendra, what did you do on this weekend away or this period of time that you were on your hiatus/recovery act?"

Kendra laughed and grabbed at her hair and said, "Well I should not say because it was not all good what I did but here goes. I actually went with my girlfriends to a ladies night strip club just to get away from the everyday sitting alone crying and disgusted feeling you get when your personal feelings don't feel right. I was invited so I went."

Kendra continued, "I had a few beers and had a great time with my girls. I was not driving so I had fun, danced and just hung out. I met a great guy that night and he was fun to be with, no drama and no ultimatums like I had with my boyfriend earlier that day."

Kendra sighed and sat back in her chair and continued, "I then did something real crazy. Maybe it was the beer or just my emotions but I asked this nice guy that I had so much fun talking too and hanging out with to take me home that night. I

Blue Ball Syndrome

know it was crazy but, I wanted to have a good time with this guy and I wanted intimacy from someone who could make me feel good right at that moment. I wanted to be held and satisfied the only way a woman fed up needs to be satisfied when her man hurts her or pushes her to the limit in a relationship.

I wanted to get back at my boyfriend and also test my own inner feelings to see if I would even miss my boyfriend. So I tested myself by sleeping with someone, like a complete stranger. I know the man that night did not obviously care about me, but he wanted what I wanted right then and there and that was a good fuck - just a great satisfying one night stand to release from the bullshit of a daily stressful life, you know."

I replied, "yea, I can understand, so what else happened on this hiatus/recovery weekend?"

Kendra, continued, "At my home, the guy was ready to have sex with me I could tell. He was attentive to me, looking me in my eyes and just trying to stimulate the moment for sexual arousal not knowing that I was already there in my mind. For the first time, I began to think just like a man and it felt good. I did not care about who he was or where he was from, I wanted him to fuck the shit out of me right then! Let's do it, come one let's do it is what I told the guy. Take off your clothes and I'll take off my clothes as well. We kissed and fooled around, it was fun."

Kendra continued, "It was like a different me experiencing all of this and I know it was wrong but at the time I did not care. I just did not want him to stop making me feel good that night. The guy asked if he could perform oral sex on me. I said yes and guided his head down between my thighs. The guy kissed my thighs good and sucked my breasts as he went down to my vaginal area, I could feel his warm tongue caressing my thighs and eventually even my vaginal area and he did not hesitate, he wanted to make me cum and he did with every lick of my vagina. I was hoping that he would do that anyway because I just wanted it like that, you know."

Greta, chimed in and said, "Girl you are bad but I can feel you on that for real though, ain't nothing like getting a man to take care of that thang, girl!" Two women laughed and seemed to know just what that moment would feel like as only women would.

Kendra continued, "I did not even think of my man through the entire time."

She sighed as if she was reliving her great night all over again as she continued. I was anxious to hear how Kendra got back with her boyfriend so I asked that she tell the group what made her go back to the boyfriend.

Kendra continued, "After that night, I took a shower and went to bed, I slept so good and I wanted to relax and unwind after such a great time. But the next morning, I awoke and it was Sunday and I remember that usually on Sundays I and my

Blue Ball Syndrome

boyfriend will hang out at the local deli market in the afternoons and catch a movie. I began to miss him and for the first time that weekend, I actually thought about him and I felt sort of bad about what I did. But, I did not feel like I needed to spill my guts to my boyfriend either.

I simply forgave myself and closed that door to that weekend experience. I enjoyed the experience and without it I probably would not have valued my love and time with my boyfriend. I actually realized that I do want him in my life and no one night stand took him away from me. I guess I had to experience that for myself and being angry at him did not help things either. So, I called him and I knew he would be at home; my boyfriend believes in resting on the weekend. I told him that I missed him and I ask what he was doing and if he would like to see me again."

Kendra continued, "I never mentioned my weekend hiatus/recovery to my boyfriend and I am sure he would never mention his time alone to me as well and maybe it should be that way. We made up and I felt good again being with him. I know he is someone stable and good to me and yes, a hell of a lover in his own right. I guess I learned how valuable he was when I learned that no one could take him out of my heart just with sex. I also learned that my heart really cares for him in the process as well. Relationships are a funny thing for sure, you never know what it is about or what you have until you know if you lost it or how you would cope without. That's what that weekend hiatus/recovery act taught me."

I thanked Kendra for sharing with the group and all the experiences shared at the group session.

It seems that many couples would agree that a weekend hiatus or a week-long trip away from stress and tension can be therapeutic to a relationship. It all comes down to the individual and what they need at the time in their lives. This does not mean that an individual has to be as extreme as Kendra was in her weekend hiatus from her boyfriend.

You may just want time to reflect, relax and return to what you see as rest and excitement in order to value your significant other even more. Furthermore, this aspect of a hiatus from a relationship or marriage is not new; it has been established as an option for couples in family counseling for many years.

Quite naturally, the practices of hiatus weekends has gained a lot of attention lately due to marital woes of celebrities, famous politicians and national sports figures that the public view as a gauge at how society is recognizing responsible behavior.

It seems that men go on hiatus weekends more than females in relationships by 47% for sexual gratification reasons. However, women are more likely to be swept off their feet and be open to an affair on their hiatus weekends by 37%. The rationale behind these findings is due largely in part to the number one thing that both sexes have stated they lack most in a relationship which is intimacy and affection. Believe it or not, the lack of these emotions actually encourages the psychological sex drive of both the sexes for sexual gratification and passion from another individual outside of the relationship.

It would only seem logical then that to avoid your lover going on a hiatus weekend for sex with someone else you should provide more affection and intimacy. This could be provided with evening walks, intimate dinners, and a date night at the movies, leaving the kids at your mom's or a babysitter.

This could also be a cruise on a ship or a romantic vacation to a nice place for the weekend. There are so many ways to increase the intimacy level of your relationship but you must find out how your significant other needs to have this expressed in order for them to appreciate your gesture of intimacy that offers a sense of satisfaction.

Lastly, if you find yourself frustrated and feeling lonely whenever your lover is around, a weekend or a week's hiatus away may be the therapy you need to find out if you really want this special someone in your life. My favorite place to recoup is somewhere warm and tropical where you can have the sun shining down on you as you lift your spirits to provide a tranquil affect on the mind and body. Or you may just decided to get a full body massage, turn the phone off and free your mind to explore the real you. Take time to enjoy yourself and return from your hiatus with a renewed mindset ready to move your relationship to the next level!

Chapter 13

WHY SEXUAL ADDICTION IS A MYTH

It seems everyone has an opinion on this age old phenomenon that is an observation of human nature that relates to our sexual appetite. Many researchers and psychologist are stating that there is some evidence that males and females can be addicted to sexual promiscuity.

However, this is quite far from the truth. Naturally, every man and woman realizes that the drive to have sex was around long before the field of psychology or the study of medicine became prominent. The drive to reproduce and have recreational sex dates even beyond biblical times.

Obviously, if the ability to reproduce wasn't possible, humanity as we know it would cease to exist. Therefore, in my opinion, to label people as addicted to sex is obviously farcical.

People are naturally attracted to other human beings of the opposite sex, eventually which leads to the production of another life. Additionally, some people even share sexual attractions to members of the same gender.

Therefore, sexual addiction cannot be defined by people who say, "I find myself wanting to have sex with someone all the time."

This statement may sound like someone addicted to sex but it is naturally based on this person's hormonal level of arousal or if the person is either male or female.

A simple smell could trigger an instant attraction to someone or even the way a man or woman looks in their clothes.

Additionally, people are also influenced by what they see, albeit an exposure to pornography or eroticism in movies, videos or whatever a person sees in their daily life. Either way, a heightened sense of smell or something visually appealing often serves as the stimulus for sex.

It seems that the more a person is exposed to a culture where sexually alluring clothing is socially acceptable, the more that men and women tend to think about sex more and more. The culture of sexual familiarity is acceptable more in an open sexual environment.

This can definitely be understood in subcultures of Europe and America where clothing is often optional on beaches and isolated communities that seem to attract men and women who believe in nudity and sexual freedom.

In comparison, this also applies for those who practice the social sexual swinging phenomenon or the sharing of your significant other sexually with other wives or husbands.   One cannot say that this is sexual addiction. It has to be merely sexual choice that avails the participants to this lifestyle.

Obviously, many couples that feel the same about their right to be sexually free but not exploited as this [is] a discreet sub-group. Swingers enjoy their lifestyle and are naturally happy with the sensual side of passion and the quest for sexual gratification that drives every sexually mature man and woman. However, not all people have access to this sexually gratifying sub-group.

It seems that sexual addiction is not an addiction at all when you break sexual access and opportunity down to which gender has more sex. This is truly the motivation of someone who will have more sex over someone else and not necessarily the inherent level of a person's own individual sexual drive.

This can be proven by the choices of sexual opportunities we make in our daily lives. Individuals that have more financial freedom to experience and engage in various forms of sexual conquest will have more social interaction with people in these subcultures in comparison with a person that does not share the same financial affluence.

Wealthy athletes, politicians, actors and celebrities consistently appear to have sexual interludes outside the norm of an average individual. These persons have what I call the "celebrity sexual magnet" for what society holds as the keys of access to just about any and all forms of sexual conquest.

It is obvious, that the glamour of fame, money and fans (of all walks of life) allow what society deems as "celebrity" to make everything about their walk of life sexually appealing to the average everyday person. In today's society, there isn't one aspect of "celebrity" that is safe from not being exposed to the sometimes unwanted advances of adoring fans.

In fact, you could stop and ask yourself, "When was the last time that you saw an unattractive woman on the silver screen as the lead actress in a romantic love based movie?"

More than likely your response would be synonymous with never. The reasons that this doesn't happen is because society loves promoting the idea of giving you an image of someone to have sex with and the illusion of an above average woman or man making love onscreen is all you need. This is by no means sexual addiction; quite the contrary, this is sexual access and knowing what the average man or woman finds to be attractive must be asked of both men and women alike.

This also helps to build the celebrity factor by engraining an imagery of what most men and women will be attracted to in society. This makes the celebrity more accessible to women or men who will avail themselves sexually to the image of arousal because of the sex appeal of this person. Moreover, most people fantasize about such an experience but rarely have access to it.

The access to sex and the financial capabilities to carry out these types of conquests are why so few people are able to accomplish multiple sexual experiences outside of their normal experiences.

Blue Ball Syndrome

The traditional days of boy meets girl and developing those warm, fuzzy feelings and living happily ever after have come and gone. Technological and telecommunication advancements via avenues such as social media and personalized video conferencing has placed sexual promiscuity at our fingertips. In a world where achieving sexual exploits was once limited by money, the gap is increasingly closing as people from all walks of life are being placed on equal sexual playing fields.

I know I am not one to judge what one does but all experts must agree it is not the addiction to sex that drives men and woman to sites like eHarmony or Matchmaker.com.

These social network sites have hundreds of people looking for that special someone to complete their view of what love, sex and compatibility is all about. However, most would agree that all the sites mentioned assist people in achieving sexual gratification or companionship, but do not ultimately lead to sexual addiction. However, one site in particular addresses the issue of sexual addiction head on.

AshleyMadison.com quotes the tagline, "why not have an affair?" and it is geared towards married people in their online community. The entire advertising campaign addresses sexual gratification, not addiction. Those who have the money, time and obviously the patience to look for a sexual experience will eventually find it on sites like these.

As one can clearly see, money is the key to the access of sex, followed by an appeal similar to celebrity status that ultimately increases one's sexual appeal to the masses.

The allure of a sexual experience with someone is the whole intent of what makes a man attracted to a woman and what makes a woman attracted to a man. It also then makes sense that as men and women achieve certain tiers of financial success, the fame and notoriety associated with that lifestyle enhances their ability to attract more opportunities to have sex and develop relationships.

This often can make one feel entitled or deserving of sexual gratification more than the average person due to the sacrifices and once previously withheld experiences that are now finally able to be achieved.

Sometimes, people feel that sexual gratification is an internal reward for their hard work after accomplishing their life's goals on a personal level. It is not common that most top-level executives and entertainers disclose their intimate private lives to the public, if they did most would agree that there would be many infractions of sexual impropriety.

After much thought and consideration, it would appear that those who achieve high levels of celebrity have to be sober in thought, action and charisma to offset the snares of the sexual predators that seek them out.

Blue Ball Syndrome

Society often blames prominent mainstream individuals such as athletes, politicians, teachers, world leaders, actors, musicians, physicians, ministers, preachers and corporate executives of "being caught with their pants down while on the job" for situations of sexual impropriety.

In contrast, people placed in the spotlight are often sought out by everyday people who will never attain their level of success or notoriety. These individuals usually are what society would consider the most apparent sexually allured people.

Seeking out these types of people have nothing to do with sexual addiction (or the myth thereof), but more so the idea of attaining something (or someone) of a sexual nature that you otherwise would never be able to attain.

The sexual acquisition of this person, once completed, empowers the person in a manner that may ultimately hinder them if they are deemed as nothing more than a conquest (not an addiction) in the eyes of the person that partook of something being willingly offered to them.

Those who seek out obvious sexual conquests of high profile people in society are the driving forces that avail themselves for sexual gratification experiences outside the norm. Overwhelming emotions may surface for everyday people that place themselves in these situations that lead to behaviors that may be detrimental for both involved parties.

Again, these types of actions should not in any way be considered as sexual addiction but another situation of a personal seeking a different form of sexual gratification. However due to the celebrity status, the possibility of developing "hooked on you syndrome" may appear.

The "hooked on you syndrome" is very powerful and leaves a person in a dependent psychological state for sexual and mental satisfaction. The person seeking the satisfaction has the power to seduce their prey at any time and at all costs in order to get what they want and have their desires fulfilled.

In the most common of terms, this can be merely described as being "love sick" without the actual presence of love being there. In these situations, person in the position of authority (in this case, the person with obvious celebrity status) will do whatever it takes to cause the other party to become so infatuated with them that this person is willing to risk it all (family, job, relationship, home, etc.) just to fulfill these momentary desires. In extreme cases, these actions have resulted in the loss of human life. It is common knowledge that there are many cases every year in which some person has been deceived into some sinister plot of spousal cheating and murder. Most of these cases are intertwined over someone attempting to achieve sexual gratification and not fulfill a sexual addiction.

It must be cautioned that a person seeking sexual gratification can be very overpowering of the person they seek and shouldn't be taken for granted. One only has to ask himself or herself, "Have I ever done anything crazy because of the love for

Blue Ball Syndrome

someone I wanted in my life?" If the answer is yes, don't be alarmed. Many are a part of this club (including myself as the author of this book).

I must point out that the seeker of the open and available person that has "celebrity status" can be either male or female. There is no sexual preference that is greater than the other. Any person in a position of authority, albeit in a local or national stage, runs the risk of being stalked by someone desiring them to fulfill sexual gratification.

One instance of such a person is someone jumping out of a private VIP room closet and surprising a male celebrity that was alone. The female stranger approached him said, "I am not here to do you any harm, and I just want to experience a moment of excitement with a famous person". The male celebrity chose to engage in a night of sexual pleasure with the woman, despite the weirdness of the situation.

The next morning, the man awoke to the woman being gone from his room. She left her contact information and email behind with a note stating, "I had a great time, please call me later." The man was on cloud nine. He tried calling her, but her calls went straight to voicemail.

He left many messages but his calls went unreturned. Day by day with no response left the man feeling exasperated and heartbroken. His world was now in a complete standstill as this woman's sexually aggressive nature had gotten his attention.

Later that night, during a scheduled dinner meeting, the man saw the unfamiliar woman that he has just spent the previous night with sitting at a table with her wedding ring on. Surprisingly, she was actually the wife to his marketing firm's CEO and looked at him in his eyes as to insinuate, "Don't act surprised, just sit down and act normal". The male celebrity watched her all night and suddenly felt uncomfortable and even embarrassed at this odd occurrence.

In a turn of events, a man that once had preyed on women had now become someone else's victim. He started to realize how she gained access to his room. The details of the experience never came out. However, the details of this sexual experience remained with him always.

Now, is it fair for us to conclude that his previous actions and lifestyle as a celebrity be deemed as a case of sexual addiction or was this merely a situation of two people seeking out sexual gratification?

You be the judge....

Chapter 14

WHY MEN AND WOMEN GET ON EACH OTHER'S NERVES

This is really an age old question that has many answers to it. Not one answer usually suffices in this area of human curiosity that opens the door to emotional or sexual dissatisfaction and motivates men and women to find another person for satisfaction in a relationship.

Let's face the fact, men and women have varying viewpoints on such a heated topic. I cannot speak for all men but I can say that guys for the most part are in agreement and we all agree that women can be very demanding when they want something from their man.

This is one thing that tops many men's list of causing problems (in addition to withholding sex). Like I said, I cannot speak for all men but the majority of them I interviewed stated, "That women have stopped or temporarily discontinued sex for a period of time when they know they want something from the man".

This is a way of controlling a man by using the power of sexual influence to do it and more often than not, it works! Some guys stated that on evenings when sexual intimacy was deprived, they were forced to sleep on the couch or in another room of the house.

I'm not talking about both parties engaging in a physical altercation, but merely a desire that a woman's needs unmet leads to intimacy being withheld.

Men may not admit that this happens more often than not and most of them will give in to a woman's requests in order for sexual intimacy to be restored. At this point, men are usually at the point of experiencing "hooked on you syndrome" and cannot resist holding out any longer.

During times such as this, women will often walk around their mate wearing little or no clothing in order to cause their mate to become extremely sexually aroused with no intent on fulfilling his desires. To further escalate the level of sexual tension in her mate, women will not even consider intimacy until the man compromises or bargains to the desires of the woman.

Most men feel that this is nerve racking and even often insulting that they have to undergo such temptation of sexual stimulation.

Obviously, feeling as if he is being made a sexual prisoner without receiving complete sexual satisfaction all because they do not agree is very problematic. Ironically, this was the number one answer men gave with regards to what women do that drive their mate crazy, especially when the woman knows the man has experienced the "hooked on you syndrome".

Blue Ball Syndrome

Most men and women can agree that significant others that take notice of another attractive person (of either sex) during mid-conversation is also nerve wrecking.

Naturally, this creates disrespect and animosity at the woman or man when this is done. It demonstrates to the person talking that they are not the other person's primary focus. Many men and women both agreed and described this tactic as being "low class" and ultimately is a social turn off which shows the character of a selfish person.

Men have been on this nerve-crazed event for years and unanimously agree that this gets on their nerves in so many ways. A man is out for a night on the town and buys a woman a drink and has a great conversation with her. They dance, share laughs, and by all accounts, appear to have a great evening. Finally, the night ends and the guy expresses that he would like to see this young lady again and she says, "Yes that would be nice" and gives him her phone number. They embrace, he respectfully, kisses her and escorts her to her car. The man is on cloud 110 by now and his spirits are soaring at this point. As he gets into his car heading home, the guy thanks the Lord for the opportunity to meet such a beautiful woman and for being allowed to have such a great time.

The next morning he wakes up and decides to call the young lady he met the night before and suddenly it happens, that terrible sound; do dong cling, goes the sound on the phone, "I'm sorry you have called a number that is no longer in service or disconnected please try your call again later, good bye".

All men surveyed said that is the worst feeling and it gets on guys nerves worse than anything because it means that you have been played by the woman that only wanted to get you to buy her a drink or she did not like you to begin with. In our opinion, that is being used in the slickest way possible and men hate this!

In contrast, women have also said that this can go both ways and they hate it when men do the same thing. But most women would agree that this usually happens to men more than women these days because men are usually the pursuers of the woman's phone number.

Men expressed that being in the mood for sexual intimacy and only to hear those dreaded words such as "Oh you have taken so long, I am not even in the sexual pleasing mood right now; I have a headache; can we do it in the morning?"

Men unanimously stated that that causes them to begin to want to look for sexual encounters from escorts to ordinary sexual conquests with other women just to have sexual satisfaction especially if this becomes a repetitive behavior by their mate. This behavior can be a demonstration of dissatisfaction of the woman with the man or a real problem of loss of attraction to the man or woman in one's life.

Blue Ball Syndrome

Women expressed having had some nerve-racking situations with men that were controversial and debatable. Let me clarify that these issues were not indicative of how all the women surveyed felt, but however, a significant portion of them.

An example of what women say got on their nerves about men is when a man states that he will be somewhere to meet a woman, gets her all excited about an event or upcoming plans, she prepares accordingly (buys a new dress, gets her hair, nails, feet done, etc.) and the man does not come through with his word of commitment. Women have stated this situation is often psychologically depressing to most women because for a woman to go to this extent of preparing herself and to be let down, it emotes a strong sense of self rejection because she literally pictured herself enjoying a wonderful night out.

Women stated that men can get on their nerves in a club or social setting when a man purchases a drink for a woman and then follows the woman around the club as if he has married the woman or taken her hostage from her intended social outing. This is a real turn off to women and many feel it is an invasion of privacy; yes, this is a big no no for women and it really gets on their badly.

Women also expressed annoyance with men who openly demonstrate flatulence, better known as passing gas! Women as a whole say that men pass gas anywhere and it is disgusting. In my study, women really said that it was at its nastiest when men and women are in bed it happens under the covers with no warning.

Unanimously, many women also stated in the study that men get on their nerves when they cannot relate to or understand the emotional feelings of their woman when women confide in them or when they are left unsupported by their man.

45% of women responded and stated that this male emotional disconnection makes a woman want to find someone who has time for her, makes her feel involved in his life and appears to be more emotionally compatible. The emotional make up of a woman is different from a man's perspective on various issues.

Women tend to be more emotional and men tend to be led more so by their physical psyche. Women pointed out in the study that most men have very little interest in the emotional stability of maintaining a healthy relationship.

In addition, women have a very hard time having sex or making love to someone that they are not emotionally involved with and compatible with emotionally. As one can imagine, this will lead to Blue Ball Syndrome in women and make any woman withdraw their attraction for sexual satisfaction away from an emotionally, absent partner that has no time for a nurturing relationship.

Survey responders point out that men and women get on each other's nerves when both are talking on the phone and tempers have escalated or

Blue Ball Syndrome

someone gets mad and then, wham.... the phone is suddenly hung up. My colleague Dana advised me that this was the worst case for both sexes because both are equally as guilty in this scenario.

I have to tell the truth and shame the devil, as older people say. I have issues when my woman gets angry with me and she hangs up on me when we are in a heated phone discussion. This causes my blood pressure to rise beyond measure because I could not have my say of the matter at that given time.

Both men and women are guilty of always trying to have to last word during a disagreement. I cannot say that it is always right to have the last word or talk. Being excessively argumentative can lead to other problems you did not plan on being there.

What I can tell you is that both sexes agreed you cannot scream at each other forever. Tension over a matter cannot consistently exist if your desire is to accomplish your goals together. This situation not only gets old but actually kills the communication efforts of the relationship over time.

Unfortunately, this breakdown of communication even interrupts sexual satisfaction and brings on symptoms associated with Blue Ball Syndrome. I have experienced this myself. I have made my many mistakes in this area.

Adversely, it was a two way mess and it took both me and my woman to clean it up by forgiving each other once tempers calmed down and we spent adequate intimate time to heal each other. In the end, we had to laugh because what we argued about on the phone was so insignificant, but we only realized this once we were calm again. Besides, it made the love making better and the kisses were sweet and real again.

Special moments were golden again, that is what is important, not the frustrated heat of being heard all the time. I know in saying this, many will identify with that and understand that it really takes an effort to restore that good vibe. Quite frankly, I would rather be at peace with my woman than at war with no love any day.

Women mentioned guys watching sports too much, ignoring them and not providing them intimacy when sports consumed the majority of their time. Most women agreed, this annoyance does not constitute leaving a relationship, but it becomes very problematic when a woman wants to cuddle or enjoy some quality time with her man and her man is hanging with the guys and watching sports all the time.

Ironically, I must play devil's advocate and point out that there are ways around this dilemma. One way around this is with a TV recording technology, like TiVo. Another remedy for a man could be to make a date with his woman where she was able to spend time with him and enjoy the sporting event as if she were still included in an important part of his life.

Blue Ball Syndrome

Men in our study unanimously agreed they disliked when women acted as if they liked a man and filled his head with all the things that he wanted to hear, but all the while, the woman is stringing him along, taking his money, enjoying going out with him but will have several other partners on the side. Moreover, when the situation comes to light, the revelation of a woman's duplicity is never a good thing for either person.

This situation can get ugly and ultimately lead to deception and betrayal on the part of both sexes. Trust is rarely restored between the affected man and woman that are caught in a scenario like this. Besides, it is difficult to trust someone that has blatantly disrespected the bond of your relationship. If taken seriously, efforts to prevent these actions can be implemented if both parties will work together for the betterment of the relationship.

The women in the study expressed problems when men make it seem like they are grandest of lovers in the bedroom however when the opportunity for intimacy arises, some men fail to satisfy their women. It was expressed that men often will touch their genitalia and even fake arousal and orgasm in an effort to prove to a woman they are more experienced in the bedroom than they really are. Some women said they were inclined to assist their partners by providing oral sex, giving him a massage or helping him to masturbate.

Ultimately, being with a mate that cannot satisfy you sexually is something that the women expressed a lot of frustration over. Frequently, the women stated that when these techniques were utilized, a man's testosterone levels increased and he was able to reestablish his sexual arousal.

This intimacy reaffirmed the evenings order for the woman's sexual needs of satisfaction to be met. In fact, the intimacy caused each person to indulge in a sexual experience without embarrassment and frustration. Many men agreed that medications such as Cialis, Levitra and the most commonly prescribed male stimulant, Viagra, have increased male endurance and stability for sex as men age.

Money is by far the most important issue that comes between a man and a woman in relationships. These problems already exist, however, with the recent economic downturn this uncertainty creates a sense of fear when attempting to date because monies are so much more closely scrutinized.

This creates problems that would have otherwise not have been an issue in previous situations. According to a divorce monitor website, the most common causes of divorce in the U.S. are irreconcilable differences due to financial problems. This demonstrates that many men and women struggle in their personal relationships due to financial familial responsibilities. Determining how to pay bills with little or no money can affect the most loving of relationships.

Blue Ball Syndrome

It seems easy to figure out the answers to one person's problems when you are not in their shoes. I will not attest to having all the answers or state that I have it all together, but I can assure you that a combination of God, prayer, communication and compromise have been the keys that have helped my relationship deal with these issues.

Arguing all the time is mentally and spiritually draining, most importantly psychologically damaging when trying to resolve any problem, particularly financial matters in a relationship. I have found that it is better to take a drive somewhere, get away with friends or family members before you say anything that can be destabilizing to that special someone or your relationship.

I have found that many couples have felt better after things have settled and they can see their way clear of a few things in order to put the essential priorities in place. Afterwards, monetary problems no longer appear to be so overwhelming.

The most challenging part of that is finding that what is important to one person may not be priority to another and this is where the selfishness and frustration interact with each other.

My own experiences as a business owner, physician and father all at the same time have demanded that I deal with these issues simultaneously. It is not always easy for me nor would it be for anyone in these types of situations.

I have had to keep a willing mind and open spirit of compromise in order to achieve my personal goals in my own professional career and especially in my home life. A good colleague and friend pointed out to me that a person with a compromising personality and a good prioritizing attitude will ultimately succeed in the matters of co-sharing the financial burdens in life that often can present a burdening effect on any relationship. In contrast, a person with a negative non-compromising attitude will inevitably bring a great relationship to its lowest existence over money.

I had to humble myself and lose the selfish attitude present in my life. I also had to do what most long term couples learned to do and that is learn to cohabitate, compromise and reevaluate my emotions and physical desires with regards to my finances in order to maintain vitality in my home and professional life. Each day, my responsibilities in that role are yet evolving.

Chapter 15

DO YOU KNOW YOURSELF WELL ENOUGH TO KNOW WHAT YOU WANT SEXUALLY

All people say they know themselves well and most people do know of what they like to eat, drink or watch on TV or what type of car they like to drive. These are abstractive objects that help shape the outside world of what we tend to think is always what people will define about a person.

However, these abstractive items will never identify the inner person that material things cannot so easily define nor are they markers to what you will come to explore in your intimate personal life.

The objects and experiences that define everything from marriage, sexual preference and romance are based on something totally different and much more in-depth in the heart of mankind itself.

It is often stated that the desires for mankind to know themselves takes a lifetime of living and experiences that ultimately shape your wants, fears and desires that only peak at levels of maturity, growth in mind, spirit and body.

For example, for a man to know what he wants from a woman may take years to discover and appreciate even though a man may have a woman for companionship for decades.

This is because men have the capacity to want and enjoy women even if they never get to know them intimately. Men are able to satisfy themselves based on their physical touch and feel nature before they consider the act of psychological registry, who the woman is or how she will fit into their world.

First priority to most men is does the woman look good, is she sexy in appearance and can she perform sexually and make me feel good in bed? Immaturity robs most young men of foundational decision making because for the first few years after puberty boys that will be men are horny guys that want to fuck and conquer their female imagery of sex appeal and the Eurocentric view point of what sex is all about.

This limits the aspect of how mature in mind a man is and it limits how he will treat a woman and this may even delay the affection for a woman as well. Many people have observed the evolution of the sexes over the years and found that women usually mature on average faster than boys/men do. Women seem to learn about themselves better than men and learn to control themselves better in social situations.

I believe this gives a woman an edge over men in their sexual maturity as well. However, just like anything else, this is not true of every woman.

Blue Ball Syndrome

Being a man, I have often wondered what attracted me to the women that I dated or found attractive in my youthful, dating days? God only knows what it could have been, maybe a length of dark lovely hair which I am still a sucker for today (I just have to be honest about that).

Maybe it could have been a smell or fragrance that really turned my head and stuck in my mind as the smell of sexual arousal and anything close to it made my hormones react to the stimulation of what my brain engrained as the drive of my manhood.

All men and women have that time that they really felt like a man or woman or a bi-sexual or homosexual experience was the event of sexual maturity and decided to attribute their lives to find out what drove them to the essence of the driving sexual force of satisfaction.

Many men and women I have spoken to over the years in developing this study and now book have always gone back to their childhood as the mechanism of their start of sexual maturity and discovery.

Quite frankly, not every experience I have run across is pleasant nor is it always easy as I have learned on a few conversations from some military buddies of mine with my time in the US Navy.

It seems that most guys start out about the age of 15 on average wondering what world the female mystic ways are to them and this curiosity, believe it or not, is already there years before but no one knows it's there. Ironically, it just is, but thank God it is not in most cases tampered with too early, if so it will denature the lifestyle of the man or woman of their mental and psychological health as they age.

Furthermore, I like to believe that in most cases the youth are allowed to grow up and be a kid and mature without the negative influences that plague on kids in our often sick society.

As mentioned, men stated they began maturity in the knowledge of women around 15 years of age; this age came up out of 140 men that I have asked over a 3 year period in my research on the topic of knowing yourself well sexually.

Men mentioned that they would get an erection for no reason if they even saw a pretty woman at that age especially around 16-18 for most guys. Men also stated that girls were intimidating to them at first and most were petrified to ask one on a date in their late teens.

Most guys are not the jocks on TV and many men had to brave their manhood in order to not seem like any punk or homosexual ("fag" or "sissy" as it was called in my young days). Homosexual behavior was not accepted in most communities and young men especially could not show any girl like features of weakness, it was not tolerated in many of the guy's days, including my own.

Obviously, now that has changed and the world is more accepting of the homosexual community. But, when I was growing up you had to be tough to show that you were worthy to be a man. Keep that shit in the closet the guys consented to say about their youth and homosexuality. However, for the most part boys were boys and all most guys agree that they wanted some sexual action not knowing anything about it, just knowing that women were hot and the world was all about getting that girl.

Uniquely, women were a little different, it seems they began around 13 or 14 years of age and I figured this was because most women around these ages started puberty and development of breast and some even menstrual periods.

These bodily changes contributed towards how a girl would go to mom and get advice on how to put on the training bras and tampons at that time of the month and learn their bodies and obviously stories of what men like about women from older women or even girls their own age.

I interviewed 136 women over a 3 year time span from all walks of life and racial diversification and most averaged their age of sexual awareness between 13 and 14 years old. Women explained to me that it seemed there was a sisterhood of development into the role of sexuality and being a woman customarily received from their moms, aunts and friends.

It seems this sisterhood educated woman on how to dress and conduct themselves and learn what attraction is and even how to grow up and knowing when guys are looking at them and how to avoid the ugly situations in life from the dangers of boys meeting girls in our society.

So now that we have started both sexes off and learned some of the early influences of both sexes, how can one answer the question of how we make our decisions of who we will select as mates within our lives?

As previously mentioned, my 3 year study asked 136 women and 140 men the same question about how they chose their mates and dates and what attracted them to their spouses and significant others in their lives? I could not believe that hardly any particular man or woman interviewed could give me a straight answer to that question. It was actually amazing because I really could not answer that question myself truthfully.

I feel it comes from the influences of expectations of what we are supposed to have in life. This expectation is based on what our parents wanted for us and what the media and movies, music, videos and books have had on our lives as we matured into manhood and womanhood over the years.

The most average answer from men was that it was how beautiful the woman was to them, if the woman was light skin or dark skin did not matter very much to most men.

Men often pointed out that if the woman was well built, had a nice grade of hair and soft hands and a nice shape she would at least catch their eyes. It would come down to their conversation and what kind of demands they would bring with the experience of the woman herself that determined if that girl would be a suitable female for the men.

The women had another way that they measured attraction in men, most women in the interview agreed that the men had to be cool and well liked by everyone and that they had to have nice hair and pretty teeth.

Women enjoyed guys that were tall and charming and flirted with them about their eyes and how the female looked on them. It seems even the young as well as the old women love to be flirted with and complimented on their appearances. Women also stated that as young girls they fantasized about guys as much as guys fantasized about them.

They were obviously better at hiding their curiosity of the guys sometime. It seems that women preferred older guys and thought that the young jock type guys were not very attractive because they were always into trouble or menacing the girls at the time and apparently that was not attractive to most women that were interviewed.

Apparently, most of the women interviewed did go on some dates usually around 17 years of age with some guys and noticed that men looked very good to them and not just high school age guys either, grown college men and athletes were the hot thing to the women in the study at this age and nothing was more of a score than to have a kiss and possibly a sexual experience with a man, not a boy at the time.

In contrast, men had their eyes on the young ladies and began to pursue the women by using all kinds of lines and sometimes trying to act cool by smoking and often driving the family car to impress the girls at 16-18 year of age.

Many of the guys had already had a first time sexual experience by the age of 17 and things were really on the maturity level of what they enjoyed about sex with a woman and when that sexual possibility would come around again.

The women began to have sex around this age as well but most admit to just kissing and fooling around until, for most age 17, and all by 18 years of age. A few women stated age 15-16, they experienced sexual activity a little earlier.

In fact, 18 women in my study had at least one child by age 21 and this was not one race of women, this was across the diverse board of the women interviewed.

Women expressed that most of the time it was about the peer pressure of fitting in with the other girls and often being accepted by the guys and not feeling like an outcast when men approached you sexually. Everybody wants to fit in and that is the pressure that most face when growing up.

I want to do the right thing but, I want to have a good time and feel good sexually with a man and not have it hurt or be a bad experience. I have the breast and the body and the taste of what sex has

Blue Ball Syndrome

felt like from previous experiences stated some women, so now to have it on the regular as in a relationship meant most women felt that they could handle that.

However, most agreed that sex education about condoms and diseases were rarely mentioned in their young days unlike the present day.

Most women agreed that to hear or say what your friends would say would be a large portion of what they got at that time about their sexual hormones and sexual maturity. Some women did have good moms and aunts and a few dads to teach them about sex, but not many.

Men on the other hand, by the age of 18-20 were the pride of sexual conquest and a man just was not a man until he had some pussy or hitting some ass is the language most guys use to describe their young conquest in the latter teen years of manhood.

Guys often recall missionary position sex and learning how to put it in and often not really knowing what the hell they were doing. Ironically, the girl regularly would have to guide the penis into her vaginal canal to keep the high aroused young man from rubbing abrasions around her vaginal area. Men laugh at that reality but it is the truth, for real.

It is also at this age when guys find out that they have not learned a lot about sex either and experiences of sex is all one will most likely have truthfully because most guys did not have an older mentor or educator to teach them the ropes of life.

It is often said that when you compare men to women and their level of sexual educational knowledge, there is a real lack of sexual awareness between both the sexes.

I have to agree as a man and author of this book, I too did not have much sexual education, just the simple birds and bees, but not about condoms and disease and how you treat a lady or even how to approach a woman about sexual attraction.

It was the way that most guys are raised up especially with strict Christian Church backgrounds and influential parents that felt that if we do not expose the youth then they will not be influenced sexually by the world and that is simply not true.

I was a complete nerd and novice, innocent but ultimately ignorant of the ways of manhood to womanhood. It was my last year of high school, my graduation year that I learned about Planned Parenthood and condoms and what some sexual education really looked like in my community, even though women were beginning to come to high school pregnant at that time.

It was strange to see a girl pregnant at 17 years of age in high school, it was not an epidemic as it is today then but I was shocked when I first saw a girl pregnant, it was like seeing an alien for the first time.

Most guys agree around 17-20 the world changes and sex is the ultimate stimulant in your mind at this time in life.

More importantly, now that the sexes have all matured into men and women in their adult life as early 20 something year olds, the question is who do you chose to enjoy your sexual maturity with?

Who will be willing to be patient enough to allow one to learn on the job and not make you feel like a dumb ass when I do not know how to make it swing from side to side or have sex from the back or perform oral sex on a woman?

Most guys know nothing about that at this young age, only what they may have seen on the porno movies and usually it is a white man performing oral sex on a white woman and making her scream and moan and do all sorts of positions that look great, but they wonder if their limited sexual knowledge will measure up.

Therefore, I am really hoping a woman is very understanding to my lack of sexual education and experience.

Consequently, as most guys, I still want to have sex even though I know nothing about it, I have a drive or an urge of instinct to be attracted to a woman and most guys agree that it is this inherent ability to be attracted to women that naturally make their selections of what they finally like sexually to please them at this mature age of readiness.

This age of influence from all aspects of manhood has finally arrived about 20 years of age. It is now we can begin to finally fully experience sex for what it is and some good sexual action and gratification from women while learning how to perform.

Women as well at 20 years of age are ready for sex and mature in every way and most have at least had some sexual experiences already for the first time, but most women agreed that it was not the best sex in the world.

Obviously, it was child's play fooling around with some head penetration with the basic missionary style positions and sometimes oral sex, but nothing many women stated that was mind blowing at their earlier ages and some even wished that they would have waited because it was not a great experience. No excitement, no fireworks went off or stars came out in the sky, according to most it was a bland innocent non-orgasmic experience.

Women stated that being older also for most meant college and living away from home for the first time. This made women more independent from their parents home so attending parties and having a private place for sex was more available and the selection of men was way more apparent to them. This raised the bar of the potential for sex and the enjoyment factor of a woman's independence of sexuality seems just as liberating as the act of sex itself.

Most women agreed that sex with a man in their more mature young years such as early twenties

Blue Ball Syndrome

was much more enjoyable and better because they were more independent and by now most knew their bodies well and what they liked about sex and how they enjoyed sex as well.

Many women evaluated the early twenties like a sexual revolution as if the flood gates of potential hot male stallions were available and everyone wanted a piece of the action.

Women stated that guys were always insinuating for sex and consistently flirting and trying to win the moment of a conversation or attention for the women and the ladies loved it, especially when at home since according to some women that was not allowed or condoned by how they were reared.

Most guys now began to see the beauty of the women and the attractiveness that the sexually endowed women brought to the table with the mature breast, nice bodies lovely hair and great skin tone. Men also liked the ass that most ladies had in college and really noticed the conversation was totally different.

According to most guys the females were open and ready to experiment sexually with a good guy that had some game or good conversation and treated the girl with some respect. It was a given that you would at least get a kiss and a phone number at this time of life and some guys talked about how the women were often the initiators of the sexual activity between them and how often women were more aggressive when it came down to sexual satisfaction.

The men pointed out that at this time there was no bills due except college tuition and nobody had any kids in college, everyone knew about contraceptives like condoms and birth control at this age as well. Most guys were glad to have a great sexual experience with a woman; once again it was the thing to do. Most of the guys in the study mentioned that missionary was the standard position and penetration from the back was a favorite for most guys as well.

All men unanimously stated that oral sex was huge on their list, this was mostly from their influence from porno movies which illustrated women performing oral sex on men and swallowing the ejaculate from the man.

All men love the idea of a woman sucking on their dick or penis like a porno star. I have not interviewed one guy that did not like that and all guys interviewed stated, "they preferred a woman that was able to perform oral sex and swallow the cum from their excited moment more than a woman that was not confident in giving a good blowjob".

Some even stated that you can tell if your woman is really into you by the way she performs oral sex on her man. If she really likes you and feels comfortable she is ever pleasing, like licking ice cream from a cone and caressing the man's dick as if it is the last dick in her life and swallowing cum is a real turn on for all men anyway.

Blue Ball Syndrome

Women who can do that are always on the top of the list with most men. It seems that by most men's accounts of their sexual experiences, mature white women are the best at performing oral sex and seem to really like it compared to other women, this was the same as with the guys in my study.

Obviously, this may not be true for all mature white women and all men may not think that but the majority of men participating in this study agreed with that. Many attributed their influence of this to be based on the porno industry where white models dominate and know how to perform oral sex and make it look pleasurable and good when performed on the average male.

I must admit, the porno industry does profile more white women than any other nationality sexually as persuasion on society, men of all races love a sexy well-built sexually stimulating white woman on film that makes sex look natural and all guys get excited watching them perform the swallow the dick technique both on screen and in reality.

Now as the author of this book, I do not want to show bias toward any woman over another sexually. I cannot say that white women are better than any other women performing sexual acts. But, I will say it is up to the individual woman and her ability of experience to please her man; in fact, all women have the potential to be sexually alluring to the man that they desire.

Women also have their own preferences of what they liked as well with men and it was obvious to me that women also enjoyed men that were well learned and experienced in pleasing them sexually. Most women in the study expressed that they enjoyed men to perform oral sex on them as well. Women acknowledge that this stimulation makes them have an orgasm just as the man will be ensured of his ejaculation.

Women stated that as men have sexual stimulation and satisfaction, women wanted sexual satisfaction as well. Women also stated unanimously that they desired a man to be intimate with them and give a good sexual performance usually missionary style that feels good to most women in the study, also the back position of the vaginal canal was a desired position that most women enjoyed with their man.

What I found out is that most women loved their men to hold, kiss and cuddle with them after the sex is over. This is a plus for most women. Women did not want the man to have this sexual experience and leave immediately right after sexual activity.

Women unanimously agreed it makes the moment feel cheated when men leave right after sex and not hold or cuddle with them. In this segment of this chapter we have discovered a sample of what men like and desire and also what women like sexually from men as well.

Now we can look at what attracts us to each other and stimulates our ability to see one man or woman over the other.

Most men like women that are at least 5'7" tall. Men feel that this height gives a woman long legs and a slender frame and a perfect height for standing next to the man. It feels good to most men to have a nice framed woman that is not fat or obese but also not anorexic or skinny either, slightly curvy and sexy but not robotic in movement. All men love a woman that looks like she can work it out well to them, it is a sign of fertility and attraction of her sexual maturity.

Women like a tall man about 5'10" up to 6'0" in height. Women stated that they preferred a man with mild brown skin or tan and some liked a man according to their preference of how he would treat the woman, some participants preferred darker complexion men based on individual criteria.

Women liked men with broad shoulders, confident cheek bones and somewhat muscularly tone in build. Women like a guy with full lips and a greatly curved ass as some of the participants pointed out.

Women seem to like a man with a slightly deeper voice which most women actually found soothing and comforting to them. Women also enjoyed a guy that has big hands and a warm body to cuddle with.

Most guys seem to like women that had soft natural complexion with tan and brown complexion being the preference of most men. Men stated that the exotic Latina women representing Dominican Republic, Colombia and South America are some of the most beautiful women in the world.

Most guys liked long hair and well built bodies with measurements of 34"-26"-34" being the most desired body shape. White women were also quite attractive, but when most men in the study had a fantasy, they often thought of an exotic, lovely woman on a beach on a beautiful tropical island, this woman was usually a woman of Latin decent.

As the author of this book, I do not advocate bias toward any man's or woman's personal preferences. It is all what a person is attracted to and what attracts men to women and vice-versa women to men.

A lot of older females prefer younger guys usually between 15-25 years their junior, in age. Women stated that after separation or divorce, they were looking for a renewal for sexual pleasure in their lives. Older women agreed that the young man's youth is fun and energetic to the women that are looking for fun, fucking and an outgoing personality to be with.

Some women knew other women that married younger men called the Cougar Effect Syndrome. I say go for it because an older woman in her forties or older is not over the hill, she is just right on the plateau of life for the eye of a young, horny man that is looking for stability, maturity and a woman that knows how to work it and provide sexual satisfaction to the man.

At 40 and older most women are pros and the years of experience is like aged wine that has gotten better with time; especially, when a woman has taken good care of herself and can still attract a young 20-30 something year old male, this is an achievement and men should just be ready for the Cougars in our society.

The population of women to men over 40 now is 5 to 1, favoring young men if they are bringing what the Cougars want. (Go for it girl, let your wild ass go for it, work that young man to death)! Get it girl: I swear there is nothing like a good seasoned woman that knows how to lay it down.

In conclusion, it seems that mankind is evolving more and more to see what attracts men to women by way of the internet and social media sites that put us in closer proximity to each other than at any other time in history.

It stands to reason that if you have a preference of what you like and go against what you really want, you are unfortunately setting yourself up for a disappointing moment in your life and in the lives of others.

For this reason, I urge all men and women to analyze, for their own sake, what they really want sexually, emotionally and physically from an individual in their relationships.

In order to do this successfully, one must first get to know exactly what they want and not stray from the preference that has been outlined in the mind of the individual. For example, if a man likes white woman, then he should try to date white women even if he is not a white man, the same applies to a woman that is of color as well.

Also, if a woman likes a well built tall, dark and handsome guy, then she should not settle for short, fat and bald because she will eventually be very disappointed in her selection because she will always covet the tall, dark and handsome man. She will seek this type of guy even with the short, bald and fat guy that loves her.

Men that are attracted to light skin African-American women should not try to make it work with a beautiful dark complexion woman, this will make them covet after light skin females because this is what they were attracted to all along. It will lead to the heart break and devastation of spirit of the dark complexion woman when the man decides to cheat with what he desires to have in the first place. Men who like Latina women from Colombia, Dominican Republic, Argentina, etc. must try to find their likeness in America or travel where those women live.

This allows access to what you desire, if not you will always look for what your sexual desires crave, even if you marry or date someone close to what you want sexually.

Men will not be satisfied and women will not be sexually satisfied as well in the intimate desires of what you want in life.

Blue Ball Syndrome

Above all, be honest with yourself and focus on how you feel attracted to someone only from your point of view only. Sexual attraction and knowing yourself is the key toward staying with a woman if you are a man and staying with a man if you are a woman. It is truly a testament when someone is emotionally, physically and sexually compatible with their significant other, husband or wife.

For example, if a man does not sexually satisfy a woman and leaves her continually hanging or waiting to enjoy her passion with her man, that man will soon be replaced by a side man if the woman does not leave totally, or even permanently replaced by another man entirely. Ironically, this man will satisfy the woman from head to toe with all aspects of sensual romance to the customary door opening customs of a well trained unselfish guy that likes to please his women.

Men who date women and love good missionary style and having sex from the back and strapping the thighs of his woman on his shoulders for deep gentle penetration in his woman should not get with a woman that cannot provide a man with that type of loving.

Furthermore, any man with a woman that does not like to perform oral sex to please her man as he likes is not good because if the man marries that woman he will come up empty handed. This man's sexual inner most desires will not be met by his unwilling wife and this will lead to unfortunate cheating that could have been prevented with the right choice of a sexually compatible mate. Most of what I have experienced from my research of living and talking to men and women all over the world is that sexual satisfaction is essential for psychological, mental and spiritual growth of couples and people as a whole.

Blue Ball Syndrome can be avoided and life can be beautiful with someone you really love and not just settle for. Do not settle in your love life or your sexual satisfaction for anyone. You have one life to live; try to find some happiness, peace and the enjoyment of life.

Life is a journey with ups and downs why should our selection of your sexual preference be so overwhelming that we cannot even enjoy our most intimate activity of our human existence. I have learned from this book to be honest, live well, enjoy my life and explore myself of what I am happy with. I am thankful in my life and I am opening my mind for the best sexual satisfaction that my woman has prepared for me and I for her.

I am all about sexual satisfaction, giving and receiving, it's all about what makes life good and knowing yourself and what you want sexually, this is the key to internal happiness in life. Find someone to love and love them based on the real you from your heart and soul.

Love is not easy but I have found that love is worth it especially when you know yourself and have found out what true love is. True love is knowing yourself and staying away from Blue Ball

Syndrome so that you can control its effects on your life. True love knows your sexual nature and your wants, your fears, what you really want out of life and how you do not want negative distractive people ruining your life. Every man and woman I know and have ever talked to seems to always look for some form of happiness in their daily lives.

If you take one day to simply be honest with yourself about what you want in your life, who you love in your life and how you feel about your life or the changes you have to make in your life, then life itself will grow and love will naturally unite you with the real desires of your heart. I am glad that I know what I want in my life now, great sex with love, a great loving woman, my children & family and my medical practice.

I am so honored to have the ability to live and enjoy the wonderful times in life. I feel good right here and right now in my life. I am still working on keeping Blue Ball Syndrome from my love life but that is a daily journey that only serious lovers can take together.

Chapter 16

TEN PEARLS OF WISDOM THAT CAN HELP AVOID BLUE BALL SYNDROME

1. Always be willing to compromise your views for that of your significant other in your life, no man or woman is an island and two heads compromising is better than lonely self-righteousness any day.

2. Always try to aim for the positive things in life and do not let anyone bring negative energy into your relationship, that prevents harmony in your communication with the one you love.

3. Never be afraid to tell your lover what you want them to do to you or for you sexually. This entices all aroused couples to a higher level. More importantly, honesty is key and you can become a living fantasy.

4. Enjoy your player spouse, don't try to change them, go dancing at a nice ball or Gala. Cook at home Travel with your player spouse and let the player enjoy you. As they say, "Don't hate the player, hate the game".

Blue Ball Syndrome

5. If you are single or just getting out of a relationship or recently divorced, you never know where new life or love can be found until you check out the average guy. The average guy is merely what you want in someone, that may be what you need. Don't be afraid of no, it only means you're a yes away, go for it!

6. Forgive, Forgive, and Forgive. I cannot stress that enough; it is a daily practice that many couples need to empower in their relationships in order to keep the flame of passion burning in your relationship.

7. Take a Hiatus/Recovery weekend before you throw in the towel on your marriage or relationship. It may be the thing that restores the value in your life about your significant other. Life is short, live well.

8. Please find out what it is that gets on your lover's nerves and practice not getting on that nerve. Learn to keep aggravation down and harmony constant in your relationship and all should be well for you.

9. All couples and lovers should always pray and go to church, synagogue, mosque or temple to have a sense of worship and communication of faith with God, that helps to sustain couples in challenging times.

10. Always keep good trusting friends and family close to you when you need someone as a counselor to talk to. Friends are great assets to keep around when relationships are experiencing rough moments. Remember never be afraid to ask for help if needed. If you love your spouse or significant other then keeping a good relationship is worth it. Above all, keep the sexual satisfaction going, always. This increases affection daily and makes the value in your spouse remain priority as time enriches your love.

About the Author

Dr. John E. Bell is a Surgical Podiatrist and former University part-time professor at Strayer University in Memphis, TN. He received his Doctorate Degree from the Ohio College of Podiatric Medicine and his Master's Degree in Health Services Administration from Strayer University in Memphis, TN. He has 5 medical offices, where he is CEO of Excelsior Podiatry Clinic PLLC, an accredited business with the Better Business Bureau (BBB) of Memphis, TN.

Dr. Bell has been on numerous TV shows including: Fox 13 News Good Morning Memphis, Fox News in Baltimore, Maryland WBFF, the Ion media network TV Channel show with Tanya Dallas-Lewis in Fairfax, Virginia. He has a current commercial on NCR 24- hour news channel 3 WREG-TV Memphis. He has also been on the Jiggy Jaguer radio show, the Georg and Nakisha Blog talk radio show, The Jay Blog talk radio show, the Rev. Jesse Lewis radio show and the Prison World radio show. Dr. Bell has appeared on the Thaddeus Matthews Show in Memphis, TN.

Dr. Bell appeared this year at the Chef Eddies Restaurant for a book signing on February 11-13, 2011 in Orlando, Florida with the youth conference sponsored by the Cora Jefferson Radio Show in Orlando, Florida. He is a panelist at the National Book Club conference in Atlanta, Georgia on July 29-August 1, 2011. He also does community events in Memphis, TN such as Sisterhood Showcase, where he will appear as a premiering author of RiverHouse Publishing, LLC on June 5th and 6th of 2011.

Not only a Surgical Podiatrist and author, Dr. Bell also performs soul music and currently has a CD expected to debut in April of 2011 entitled, *Dr. Bell Special Occasion Tribute from Soul to Soul.* He will be in concert as a new Neo-Soul music artist on June 25, 2011 at the historic New Daisy Theatre. On June 25, 2011 Dr. John E. Bell debut his live performance in Memphis at the 103.5FM Family day reunion concert at the Overton Park Levitt-Shell Theatre in Memphis, TN before over 3500 citizens in Memphis, TN. Dr. John E. Bell has toured in Europe with his Soul music in Holland, Amsterdam Muzicafe November 29, 2011 and In London, England (UK) at the Finsbury House of Live music in London, England (UK) November 30-31, 2011. Dr. Bell has a new Soul music CD entitled "Dating Again released in 2012. This music album is the Soundtrack for "The Internal Mist of Love". This soul music artist is heard all over the world on multiple BDS radio, internet and satellite radio stations. Dr. Bell currently resides in the Metropolitan area of Greater West, TN, has one daughter, and is a proud member of Phi-Beta-Sigma Fraternity Inc.

For more information, visit www.drjohnebellbooksandmusic.com.

Music CD site: www.cdbaby.com/cd/drjohnebell12

Invasion of the Baby Daddy

EVERY UNWED MOTHER'S NIGHTMARE COMES TO LIFE IN THE PAGES OF INVASION OF THE BABY DADDY, a compelling and moving debut novel that echoes the emotional and cerebral frustrations of unwed mothers throughout the ages. Its unforgettable characters and authentic story line are interwoven with current and real facts about the volume of unwed mothers in our society today.

In the story, Dr. Sands believes he has found his perfect mate only to discover that she is pregnant from a previous relationship. Not fully aware of the ramifications of this colossal news, Dr. Sands and Rachel date via long distance during her pregnancy and ultimately decide to get married. In order to make a life together, Rachel must move to Tennessee to start a new life with her husband. But the Baby Daddy has other plans for them. Determined to make this marriage work, Dr. Sands goes to extraordinary lengths to try and negotiate with the Baby Daddy. Brimming with honesty from the author s own experiences, Invasion of the Baby Daddy comes alive with unique freshness, candor and rich detail.

ISBN-10: 0615336116

ISBN-13: 978-0615336114

Retail Price: new price $9.99

I Think I Can Be A Doctor

The story about Jeremy is a great story that will inspire all children at ages 9 and up and even adults as well. This story takes place in a young boys life as he decides on what he wants to do with his life. Jeremy is from a disadvantaged background and takes notice of many negative images around him but he has a great mother and a loving home life that motivates him to want more in life for himself. Jeremy loves the health shows on cable TV and really wants to become a Physician or someone in the health care field that he admires on the weekly discovery health shows he enjoys so much. One day by pure coincidence Jeremy has a unique accident and Jeremy is taken to the hospital. It is here where he lives through everything that he has seen on TV and meets the people that will forever change his life and certainly will make an impressive impact on his future. Do not miss this inspiring and heart felt story based on real life events about a boy named Jeremy from humble beginnings that gets more than a medical treatment from his accidental fall. Jeremy gets a mentorship that will inspire him to achieve his goals throughout life. I hope you enjoy and are inspired by this book to encourage our children to excel and achieve in school by believing in themselves for positive goals that can be achieved. This can happen when our children can be mentored to believe that they too can say, "I think I can be a Doctor" ISBN: 978-0983218609 price $9.99

Do I Fit the Color of the Rainbow?

In the book, "Do I Fit the Color of the Rainbow?" the reader will find a great book that reflects the existence of every day human life, often referred to as the Color of the Rainbow of thought. This concept evolves from a professional African-American male's perspective, which is quite engaging and incredibly honest about life's challenges and blessings. The book shows a unique insight on topics from the cultural trends of African-Americans to what's going on with relationships considerably marriage/divorce from an urban stand point. Dr. Bell intimately allows the reader to be ringside while experiencing a family in the Internal Mist of situations and dares to ask, what would you do? Incredibly, the reader gets a great sneak peek inside the men's locker room to hear what frustrates men with relationships according to a 3-year study performed by Dr. Bell. Don't miss this great book of American urban fiction with a twist of reality truth as only the mind of author Dr. John E. Bell can present it.

ISBN-10: 0983218633

ISBN-13: 978-0983218630

Retail Price: $9.99

Please Visit My Social Websites below and I greatly appreciate your support of my books and my Soul Music CD album and single. I thank you all from the bottom of my heart.
Dr. John E. Bell

1.) Music site: www.cdbaby.com/cd/drjohnebell5
2.) Music site: www.reverbnation.com/drjohnebell
3.) Facebook:www.facebook.com/drjohnebell
4.) Twitter: twitter@authordrjohnebell
5.) Music site: www.cdbaby.com/cd/drjohnebell12
6.) Internet radio: jango.com type in Dr. John E. Bell
7.) Tunecore.com
8.) itunes.com

www.ingramcontent.com/pod-product-compliance
Lightning Source LLC
Chambersburg PA
CBHW031348040426
42444CB00005B/226